GRS 20

16/20

A Mix
of Years

Also by
William S. Morse

A Country Life

Cover:

Bill Morse in 1915 (age 10) & 1995 (age 90)
on the summit of Mount Moosilauke,
Benton, New Hampshire.

Painting by M. C. M. Havens
Mt. Moosilauke Summit House
June 12, 1933
Courtesy of the Dartmouth Outing Club

Some Responses to

A Mix of Years

"To read William Morse's *A Mix of Years* is to step back in time to a period when nothing came easy for anyone. As Bill relates, the rewards of such an existence are appreciated only later in life.

"Bill Morse is a wonderful storyteller, and what an assortment of tales he has to tell! The many characters he has come across in his life — from Ai the eccentric woodsman to Charlie, the Russian lumberjack — provide the author with a book full of humorous, interesting anecdotes. *A Mix of Years* is the next best thing to visiting with Bill himself. His colorful anecdotes of summer life atop Mount Moosilauke, working the woods of New England's vast forests, and growing up in the hill country of the upper Connecticut River valley are colorful, enlightening, poignant. His commentary on life here in the latter stages of the twentieth century is also remarkably perceptive and accurate.

"If nothing else, *A Mix of Years* is a celebration of this New England Yankee's first 93 years of life. And it's been a life many of us probably wish we'd had the privilege to live."

— **Mike Dickerman** – White Mountain hiker, historian
Author of *A Guide to Crawford Notch* and
Along the Beaten Path.

"The wealth of detail, wisdom and humor that comprises *A Mix of Years* is priceless. Whoever reads it will enter on an unforgettable journey that will take them through the early years of our New England way of life. It could only have been written by a man of Bill Morse's years. Years that have been lived wisely and well.

"*A Mix of Years* is a doozy. It places William S. Morse on center stage as a gifted New England historian, philosopher and humorist. What a gift he has for storytelling."

— **Floyd W. Ramsey**
Author, *Shrouded Memories*

"Bill Morse has done it again. His recollections of Pike, East Haverhill and Bean Hole Beans are as bright as a June sunrise over Mount Moosilauke. A wonderful book... required reading for North Country folks. His descriptions of storms on the mountaintop just might drive you under the bed to escape their fury."

— **Bernie Marvin**
Publisher, Northcountry News-Independent
Haverhill Corner, N.H.

"... a good read to any fan of New England lore. Many of the book's characters seem to jump right off the page."
— **Kristin Bloomer**
The Rutland Herald

"Bill Morse is a North Country treasure — *A Mix of Years* is the mother lode! It's like sitting on the veranda listening to your great grandfather tell about life in northern New England in the first half of the century. You are enthralled, not wanting the stories to end."
— **Gary W. Moore**
Columnist, free lance writer
Bradford, Vt.

"Bill Morse's long career in field and forest provided him with sage insights on the interactions — sometimes positive, sometimes negative — between humankind and Nature. Reading Bill Morse's reflections will give readers a step up and a step ahead in understanding Life, even if they have never held a peavey or swallowed a dose of Troutman's Cough Syrup. He has the historian's eye for lively detail and the sociologist's awareness of what makes the world work, for better or worse. He introduces us to "natives," not all of whom are model citizens and not necessarily colorful or even pleasant to deal with.

"I had soot in my eye and cinders in my shoes after reading his account of a pre-World War I train journey to Boston from East Haverhill, New Hampshire. I understand the hierarchy of the logging operation and its almost lost terminology — boom logs and watermen; scalers, drivers, jobbers, wood butchers; the dingle and the hovel and the wangan. Paul Bunyan is no legend.

"Bill's compressed record of the famous 1938 New England hurricane is excellent history, but his version is particularly significant in balancing the well-known disaster and tragedy with the less well-known "silver cloud" that floated, over northern New England especially, for years afterwards. For many men and their families struggling to survive in the depths of the Depression, those windrows of fallen trees, those tangles of trunks and roots and branches, represented wished-for and unexpected employment: literally, a windfall of jobs in the woods and sawmills. The forests may have been flattened, but the economy, for many, bloomed and blossomed.

"Mr. Morse, as he did in his earlier book, *A Country Life*, gives us his tough North Country world, "warts and all," without sentimentality and with a wry Yankee humor."
— **Alan N. Hall**
Hopkinton, N.H.

❄   ❄   ❄

A Mix of Years

by William S. Morse

Moose Country Press
1998

Moose Country Press
Warren, N.H.

ISBN 0-9642213-5-7

Library of Congress Cataloging-in-Publication Data

Morse, William S. (William Sanders) , 1904–
    A mix of years / by William S. Morse.
      p.   cm.
    ISBN 0-9642213-5-7 (pbk. : alk. paper)
      1. New Hampshire--Social life and customs.
2. Vermont--Social life and customs. 3. Morse, William S.
(William Sanders), 1904– 4. Haverhill (N.H.)--Biography.
5. Loggers--New Hampshire--Biography. I. Title.
F39.M67   1997
974.2'043'092--dc21
[B]
                                        97–26811
                                        CIP

10 9 8 7 6 5 4 3 2

Printed in the United States of America

Dedication

A book is like a ship that requires
someone at its helm to guide it
on its launching and on its voyages.
This book is dedicated to Robert W. Averill
in appreciation for his helmsmanship
that resulted in the launching of it
and my previous book, *A Country Life.*
Without Bob there would have been no voyage.

A Mix
of Years

Contents

Mountain Years
Commentary — Stearns A. Morse

Forest Years
Commentary — Paul T. Doherty

Illustrations

William S. Morse —
    Sketches — 3, 16, 24, 35, 54, 60t, 61, 67, 75, 91, 93, 124, 126, 165,
               180, 187, 201, 208, 223
    Photos, etc. — 104, 112t+b, 116, 118t, 133, 135, 137, 191, 192, 197, 198

New Hampshire Historical Society — 4, 10, 28, 38, 63, 176, 207
Warren (N.H.) Historical Society — 19, 22, 96, 98, 169
Haverhill (N.H.) Historical Society — 77

Boston Public Library — 106
Dartmouth College Baker Library — cover painting
Greenfield (Mass.) Public Library — 60b, 68

Benton, N.H.
    J. Willcox Brown — 166
    Henry Merrill — 149

Berlin, N.H.
    Paul Charest — Morning Lane Studio — 171, 172t+b, 196, 210, 211
    Peter Rowan — Northern Forest Heritage Park — 177, 190

Haverhill, N.H.
    Edwin Blaisdell — 49, 51, 52, 57, 70, 71t, 73, 74, 173, 200

Lyme, N.H.
    Scott Nichols — 168
    Pauline Whittemore — 174

Rutland, Vt.
    Vyto Starinskas — Rutland Herald — 222

Warren, N.H.
    Esther Whitcher — 25, 26, 46, 69, 71b, 80, 81, 84, 86, 90, 110b,
        122, 128, 193t+b, 217t+b, 219, 220
    Marjorie S. Davis — 144, 203

Additional illustrations — collection of the publisher (RWA).

Foreword

Kristin Bloomer of the Rutland Herald interviewed Bill Morse in June, 1997, and adeptly explored the author's approach to writing:

"I just bring up past memories, more or less to pass away the time, bringing some of the past to life as it was — it gives <u>me</u> life. I also also wanted to inject a few things that would give people food for thought, without sermonizing... to make people draw their own conclusions."

❄   ❄   ❄

There are, perhaps, a few other sharp Yankees in their nineties whose memories are impressive and who write well and with a sense of humor. Bill Morse stands alone, however, with his particular mix of rural Yankee heritage, boyhood summers atop Mount Moosilauke, careers as a surveyor and logging boss, and colorful characters encountered.

In the course of his writing, he chronicles many changes of the twentieth century. The boy who turned eleven on Moosilauke in 1915 and whose winter home was a farm in the valley below regarded automobiles, telephones, and electric power as novelties. Eighty years later the same boy again stood on the summit, gazing out across the vastness and remembering; traveler and eyewitness on the long road from the nineteenth century to the twenty-first.

Jack Noon
Editor
Moose Country Press

Acknowledgements

Many people have lent a hand in the creation of this book.

Jere Daniell, Tony Morse, Will Lange, and Paul Doherty provided their special North Country perspectives in their commentaries introducing each section of the book.

Illustrations were selected from many sources — historical societies, libraries, and private collections. Esther Whitcher of Warren, N.H., has provided some of the most telling images of life in a small New England town to go with Bill's recollections. The unique collection of Edwin and Katharine Blaisdell of North Haverhill, N.H., supplied the many blacksmith and logging tools, patent medicines, and other items from the past.

Additional people who should be thanked include Ruth Jeffers Wellington, Lee Kryger, June Klitgord, Victor and Vesta Smith from the Haverhill Historical Society; Bryan Flagg, Harriet and Grover Libbey, Lyle Moody, (and others) from the Warren Historical Society; Sherry Wilding-White and Bill Copeley of the N.H. Historical Society; Anne Ostendarp at Dartmouth's Special Collections in Baker Library; Katherine Dibble at the Boston Public Library; Paul Charest (Morning Lane Studio) and Peter Rowan (Northern Forest Heritage Park) in Berlin, N.H.; Scott Nichols and Pauline Whittemore in Lyme, N.H.; Marjorie S. Davis from Merrill's Mountain Home (and points south); master photographer, Vyto Starinskas from the Rutland Herald; Dartmouth "chubbers", Will Brown, Hank Merrill, Tom Burack, Dave Hooke, Jim Collins, Jamie Trowbridge, and Bill Keefe.

We were also encouraged by the comments of the many people who volunteered to review this work — Kristin Bloomer, Mike Dickerman, Bernie Marvin, Alan Hall, Gary Moore, and Floyd Ramsey.

Gary Russell of Burt Russell Litho (Greenfield, Mass.) took on the cover design and illustrations for the book, and provided both expertise and moral support as text and image were joined together. Tom Plain and Jan Stevens at BookCrafters guided the book through its final printing.

Robert W. Averill M.D.
Publisher
Moose Country Press

Early
Years

Introduction to Early Years

"Define the word Yankee in any way that you perceive it," Bill writes at the end of his first mini-essay, "shrewdness, hardheaded common sense, discipline, thrift, a down-to-earth sense of values, or plain cussedness — it is all Yankeeism." The "Early Years" section portrays some of the Yankees Bill became fond of while poking around in written histories of local towns, listening to stories about his ancestors, and reminiscing about his experiences as a land surveyor. The most prominent Yankee in the section, of course, is William S. Morse himself.

Characters from the past include cash-poor frontiersmen who convince a Harvard-educated lawyer to drop a legal suit against them, an ancestor who runs a tavern located along a now-abandoned road, and local folk who save the town drunk from being punished for a misdeed he may or may not have committed. Morse seems especially fond of stories with upbeat endings. The essay entitled "Caleb" begins, "Our family has been pretty free of the taint of having any politicians in it," but ends with a paragraph in which Morse's father explains why democracy works so well. "Rhubarbs" acknowledges some "deliberate Yankee manipulation" in the drafting of many land deeds. The personalized surveying stories, however, all conclude with justice well-served.

Readers won't have much trouble knowing what the author thinks about life during the early years. The sentence "A good dose of (Yankeeism) could prove beneficial to us today," terminates Bill's discussion of regional identity. "One cannot escape the feeling," he writes elsewhere, "that ... those old-timers lived a life ... in numerous ways more vibrant and full of meaning than the life many of us lead today." In the end he asks only that we appreciate the past, not romanticize it. "If you are the sort of person who likes to travel untrammeled areas, and you encounter an old piece of wall or something unusual all by its lonesome in some wild, isolated spot, observe it with respect. It may have a story to tell."

Bill Morse, at 93, writes marvelous stories about his and his forebearers' early years. Enjoy this first batch.

Jere Daniell
Hanover, New Hampshire

(Jere R. Daniell is Professor of History at Dartmouth College and is known widely as a colonial historian. He is the author of *Experiment in Republicanism: New Hampshire Politics and the American Revolution, 1741–1794*; and *Colonial New Hampshire: A History*.)

COMMERCIAL BEGINNING OF NEW YORK.

Yankee

Just what is a Yankee? That question was asked of me during an interview with a reporter, and after some discussion we agreed that it was a poser. Put that question to a dozen people and you will likely get a dozen answers. Several might suggest that a Yankee is defined by a combination of characteristics, but then fail

1

to agree on much aside from the Yankee's hardheaded-
ness, independence, and aversion to being labeled or
defined. Webster gives several definitions of the word.
One of them is that a Yankee is a person from New
England, but that is a little too broad. Not everyone in
New England has those particular traits that are usually
attributed to a Yankee; traits that have changed and
taken on different meanings with the passage of time.
As a start to determining a narrower definition, we
should perhaps consider what we can learn about the
history of the word and the reactions of some of the
Yankee's historical victims.

Some historians say that the term originated with
the Dutch. Years before they purchased Manhattan
Island they were the first to sail up the Connecticut
River and to explore the coast along Long Island Sound;
explorations which they felt gave them first claim to
that area which became known as Connecticut. According to the rules of the game of those days they considered it to be theirs, but a bunch of malcontents from the
Bay Colony of Massachusetts began settling along the
river, and they managed to euchre the Dutch out of
their claim. According to one version the Dutch called
the squatters "Jankins," which was their word for
"Johnnies." Another version states they called them
"Jan Kees" (John Cheese). Whichever it was, the Dutch
pronounced the letter J as we pronounce the letter Y,
and the settlers became known as "Yankees." So, as far
as the Dutch of those days were concerned, a Yankee
was a person from Connecticut who was hard to get
along with, and was one who could euchre a person out
of house and home. One had to be careful when dealing
with him. In a short time the word Yankee was applied
to the inhabitants of the rest of New England.

The settlers along the Connecticut and other
rivers were hard workers. They cleared the land for

their farms. They were thrifty, and were soon producing more than they needed. They were also industrious and inventive, and they began tinkering around and producing things that other people might need. They had to find a market for their products, and a lot of them became peddlers, traveling the interior of the country peddling their wares. At first, when there were hardly any roads, they traveled on horseback, and some traveled the rivers peddling their goods from boats. When the roads were improved they loaded wagons and became traveling stores, penetrating the country to the north, west, and south. To those people whose countryside was being invaded, a Yankee was a peddler from Connecticut hawking his wares, and was a person whose scruples would bear watching. According to some reports the people who bought his nutmegs found many of them to be made of wood; the pumpkin seeds that he sold could run heavily to wood chips; and his pepper had a tendency to be well diluted with colored sawdust.

Those who sought wider horizons took to the sea with shiploads of their wares. They traveled to foreign shores where they traded their cargoes for rum, molasses, sugar and other products which were unloaded at good prices when they returned home. They competed with a similar breed of mariners from down east who

3

Yankee Mariner's Compass (c. 1750)
"Made and Sold by Joseph Halsy
Boston, New England"
N.H. Hist. Society #F2486

were known as Maine Yankees, and they shared foreign
ports with ships of Yankee merchants that hailed from
Massachusetts and Rhode Island. A shrewd sea captain
could pay for his ship in a couple of successful voyages,
and in foreign ports a Yankee was known as a sea-faring
man who was a shrewd, hard-headed trader.

Vermont and much of New Hampshire were
settled by Yankees from Massachusetts and Connecticut. Those who chose Vermont were lured to the place
by an avaricious Yankee who was the Royal Governor
of New Hampshire. He granted and sold them land in
the form of townships: land to which he had dubious
title. According to New York's charter the land that he
sold belonged to them, and they became embroiled in
a heated, war-like controversy with his grantees, who
were led by Ethan and Ira Allen, two contumacious
Yankees from Connecticut. The hard-headed settlers
refused to be ousted from land which they had paid for,
and to New Yorkers a Yankee was a Vermonter who was
stubborn and who was a disciple of the Devil.

4

Even in those early times, the term Yankee had a different meaning to different people. Not all Yankees were predatory traders or peddlers. There were farmers, merchants, lawyers, tradesmen, and other professionals, who were endowed with the Yankee characteristics of hard-headed common sense, thrift, and aggressiveness. Some were undoubtedly parsimonious, and a few of them may have had a touch of larceny in their souls, but most of them were upstanding citizens who played a strong role in shaping the birth and course of our country. They were strong believers in the rule of self-preservation and independence, and were resentful of too much regulation and taxation by their rulers in England; enough so, that they fomented a revolution. Present day Solons should take heed.

Fourteen Yankees signed the Declaration of Independence for the New England states, and in the war

A Minute man.

that ensued the rebellious inhabitants of all the thirteen colonies became damned Yankees to King George and the British. During our Civil War, all of the Northerners were damned Yankees to the Confederate states, and even today anyone north of the Mason Dixon line is a damned Yankee to some Southerners.

Five of our elected presidents were Yankees from New England. Coolidge, who occupied the White House in the 1920's, was a model of Yankee thrift and common sense. He was a Yankee from Vermont, who was so tight-lipped and taciturn that someone wrote that he was weaned on a pickle. He has often been described derisively, but his administration was the last one that presided over a period of prosperity without running the country into the hole. In fact, he provided a surplus and reduced the debt, and he did so while keeping his mouth shut and leaving things alone.

He may have been taciturn, but his observations were to the point. He told Bernard Baruch: "It is necessary to watch the people in Washington all the time to keep them from unnecessary expenditure of money. They have lived off the government so long that they are inclined to regard it as a Christmas tree, and if we are not careful they will run up a big expense bill on us."* His observation seems to have been prophetic, not only of the people that we send to Washington, but also of many throughout the country.

There seems to be some evidence that the old hard shell Yankee is a vanishing breed. Yankee common sense, thrift, discipline, skepticism, self reliance and stubborn insistence on living within one's means disappeared from government and much of the country some time ago. The accepted customs of present day society differ in many ways from those of the early years of our twentieth century. There are now a couple of generations who do not realize that there was once a time when there was no such thing as public welfare, where some able-bodied people receive as much money for being idle as many of those who work trying to make ends meet; a time when people were reluctant and ashamed to accept help, and were proud enough to consider it a stigma when they had to do so. There was also a time when criminals were punished and made to pay for their crimes, instead of being coddled and benefited by the law and peddlers of liberal dogmas. They were taken out of circulation. People felt safe while

---

* "The Real Calvin Coolidge," edited by Grace Coolidge, *Good Housekeeping Magazine* (1935)

walking the streets, and everyone, young and old, had respect for the institutions and rules of society.

Define the word Yankee in any way that you perceive it — shrewdness, hardheaded common sense, discipline, thrift, a down to earth sense of values, or plain cussedness — it is all Yankeeism. A good dose of it could prove beneficial to us today.

Hutchinson

Our general knowledge of the history of our country, and of the times before and after the revolution which gave it birth, seems to be confined mainly to its leaders and to the major political events of that time. We learn to recite the facts by rote without absorbing any awareness of the spirit of the people of that era. Often, a study of local history and some of its unsung characters will reveal their strong commitment to guarding their hard earned liberty and independence. They were very zealous in doing so, as the following account will illustrate.

One of the pioneer Yankee lawyers of the Upper Connecticut Valley was Aaron Hutchinson who moved from Massachusetts to Lebanon, New Hampshire, to practice law. The valley was a pleasant place that was being rapidly settled, and he must have figured that it offered many opportunities to an enterprising Harvard-educated lawyer who was well versed in the city practice of those early days. He was described as being a courtly and well dressed gentleman, wearing knee breeches and ruffled shirts. According to the records he was one of the first three members of the Grafton County Bar, and had an illustrious career. Ethel Rock Millen in writing *Historical Sketches of Early Lebanon* quotes an account from *The Lebanonian* of 1898. This piece tells in some detail of an occasion in which Aaron Hutchinson came up against the temper of the local citizenry and appeared to come out second best. The incident occurred early in his practice, shortly after the American Revolution.

A paper was being published in Windsor, Vermont. It was distributed throughout the Upper Valley as

far north as Norwich by a post rider on horseback who was paid by the subscribers on a yearly basis. The only money that was trustworthy in those days was hard money, and the post rider would not accept anything in payment but silver. Money did not circulate very freely at that time. It was hard to come by, and when the yearly payment for the subscriptions came due most of the sorely pressed people of the area did not have enough hard money to meet the tab. The post rider had to accept notes in payment.

Upon his return down river, he went through West Lebanon where he sold the notes to Hutchinson, who immediately sued the makers for payment. The people of the area, including some who were not directly involved, were not at all pleased with the action. They considered it to be out of accordance with the spirit of the times. They had meetings and conferences and found that they could only raise about one-half of the amount of the notes in silver. They appointed a spokesman to represent them and form their response to the suit.

When the day for the hearing came around, the people formed a procession which marched to the meeting house where court was due to be held. It was evidently a motley crowd with many people in it who had fought in the Revolution, and they were led by drummers. Before the Court session officially began lawyer

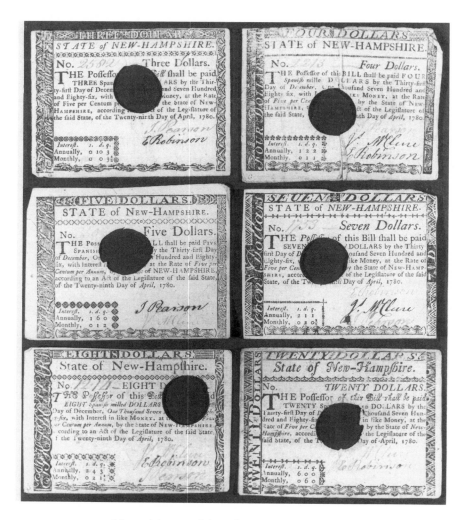

New Hampshire Currency (1780)
N.H. Hist. Society #F1049

Hutchinson was asked to appear at the door so that the people could talk with him. When he made his appearance, the spokesman for the group addressed him essentially as follows:

"Sir, we came into this country when it was a wilderness. We subdued the Indians. We subdued the beasts and the forest. We subdued and settled the land, and we recently subdued the forces of the King of England. Our biggest enemy now is the lawyers, and

10

I will tell you what we are going to do about them. We will pay you one-half the amount of the notes which you hold in silver, and you can ride your horse home. If you do not want to accept that, you will ride out of town on that horse," — and he pointed to a sturdy fence rail supported by several husky men — "and I will ride yours." After a few moments of deliberation, lawyer Hutchinson accepted the offer, and rode his horse home.

We do not know how much Hutchinson paid the post rider for the notes, but it is possible that he came out all right money-wise. It is also highly probable that he added a bit to his Harvard education by becoming aware of what Ethan Allen, the old Vermont war horse, meant when he thundered that "The Gods of the hills are not the Gods of the valley."

Stephen

Our early ancestors who settled this country must have been a hardy lot. Paying attention and homage to them seems to be of some consequence today, especially those ancestors who became early settlers of the wilderness. The descendants of those souls who endured the hardships of first clearing the land take pride in being able to trace their roots back to the pioneers. The genealogical research is not too difficult, but it does not usually reveal any knowledge of their particular characteristics; how they lived, or what they were really like. We have but little awareness of the sort of life they lived in what must have been a lonely land, and any supposition of their individual traits can only be arrived at by information obtained from town histories or from contemporary accounts.

The earliest of my ancestors to settle in our town of Haverhill, New Hampshire, was named Stephen Morse. The town history states that he came from Massachusetts, had been a soldier in the Revolution, and that he was a blacksmith. Some soldiers received an allotment of land as payment for their services in the army. Others, who were artisans, were given land as an inducement for them to settle in the wilderness. The services offered by artisans, such as millwrights and blacksmiths, were important in those early days, when travel was only by horses and oxen and when grain had to be ground into meal and flour and trees had to be sawed into lumber. Stephen might have received his land in such a manner, although there is no record of it.

Whatever the circumstances, sometime before 1780 Stephen settled on what had been the first road in town and which in those earliest years was the most traveled road leading from northern Vermont and New Hampshire to the south and the sea coast. He cleared land for a farm and with the help of one of his sons, Caleb, who bought land adjoining him, they enlarged it, and they ran a tavern in conjunction with their farming activities.

The Catamount Tavern (Bennington, Vermont)

Stephen was described by a contemporary as a jovial person who was fond of telling stories. He must have been a congenial tavern host for it is reported that he kept a big brown jug of cider warming on the tavern hearth in the winter. He had a hearing problem which made him dependent on an ear trumpet, and the tavern became known as "Deaf Morse Tavern." The road, which followed what was originally an old trail, was probably a poor apology for one, and the busiest season for the tavern was in the winter when plentiful snow provided good sledding.

During the winter season it became a popular overnight stopping place for the many drovers of the northern area who sledded their produce in one- and two-horse pungs the long distance to Boston and other cities.

An historian described the house as typical of the early taverns. Four downstairs rooms comprised the reception hall or parlor, the tap room, the dining room and the kitchen. The proprietor and his family occupied the upstairs and the attic. In those early taverns it is reported that the drovers slept on the floor in the bar room and the parlor with their feet to the huge fireplaces that contained great fires. It appears that the tavern flourished until a better and easier road was built through the valley to accommodate the stage coaches which were making an appearance. The tavern and the building that housed it eventually succumbed to the ravages of time.

The hill and the area in which the tavern was located became known for some time as Morse Hill and the Morse Neighborhood, probably due to Stephen's achievement in populating it with Morses. He sired twelve children, all of whom were boys. Twelve is a good round number, but there were some who exceeded it. Large families were common in those days. The reason can probably be explained by the story of a farmer's response when he was asked what the people in such remote places did for amusement, especially when they were snowbound in winter. The farmer answered that in the summer they fished and fiddled around, and in the winter they didn't fish.

My father's farm, where I grew up as a lad, adjoined what was once Caleb's and Stephen's farm. The records show that Caleb had nine children. If the rest of Stephen's sons were as prolific, there must be a goodly number of his descendants that are around today.

According to Haverhill and Ryegate histories, another of Stephen's sons, Robert, carried on the tavern tradition, moving to Rumney, where he evidently ran a tavern known as Morse Inn. He also was a stage entrepreneur. He organized the first stage route between Concord and Haverhill and was interested in other lines as well.

The tavern and the buildings have been long gone, but their foundations and a sizable root cellar were in evidence when I was young. Today the site is a remote, isolated area that has grown up to brush, and the road, which is devoid of any habitation and is in a sad state of disrepair, is probably not much different

Stage-coach of 1828.

than it was in the old tavern days. It is hard to imagine that it was once an important thoroughfare where there was a tavern that was the rendezvous of a bunch of boisterous drovers huddling in front of the huge fireplaces and partaking of the contents of Stephen's old brown jug.

One cannot escape the feeling that, in spite of their hardships and the crudity of their circumstances, those old-timers lived a life that was in numerous ways more vibrant and full of meaning than the life that many of us live today.

Caleb

Our family has been pretty free of the taint of having any politicians in it. There is no record of any in my mother's family. My grandfather did not have a very high opinion of them, and he used to lambaste them every once in a while. He said that most politicians were like a rooster he once owned who thought his crowing made the sun rise. He claimed that any of them could crawl through a knot hole or change their mind at the drop of a dollar. There is a record of only one in my father's family, and he died over one hundred and fifty years ago. The records of those early times are scanty, and it is difficult to tell what sort of person he was. I do not think that he had a very enjoyable political career. About the only thing the town history says of him is that he was the plaintiff in a political libel case that became famous.

His name was Caleb. He was the son of Stephen Morse, who settled in our area some time before 1780. Both he and Caleb appear in the early town records as tax collectors, but in those days, and for quite a few years thereafter, the job of tax collector was put up for bid. It was not a political office. Caleb was successful in bidding off the job for quite a few years. The bidding must have been pretty competitive. Some years it went for around four cents on the dollar, and other years it went for less than two cents. According to the deed records, Caleb's farm adjoined the northerly part of my father's farm, where I grew up as a boy. He and his father ran a tavern as an adjunct to their farming activities. The town history tells of an old Morse Tavern in that area which was used by the drovers.

Through his interest in the militia he became known as Colonel Caleb, and in 1807, when he was twenty-three years old, he was elected to be one of the highway surveyors. He was one of seven that were elected that year. They must have had one for each district. The following year he was elected as a hog reeve, and they had several of them.

There were some town offices at that time that sound strange to us today. They elected tythingmen, fence viewers, sealers of leather, cullers of staves, corders of wood and haywards. In 1825 Caleb was elected selectman for a couple of years, and advanced up the political ladder by being chosen as representative to the General Court in 1828 and 1830. At that time I suppose it was a great honor to be chosen to represent the town in the legislature. In his run for re-election in 1830 he ran afoul of the media and a person named John Reding.

Reding was a newcomer to the area who had come to town from Portsmouth and established a newspaper which was named the *Democratic Republican*. Those were the days when Andrew Jackson made his run for the Presidency, and in his second try at it in 1828 he defeated the incumbent, John Quincy Adams. Reding was a Democrat and a Jackson follower, whereas Caleb was a Whig and a devotee of Adams, who was an Independent Federalist. It seems that the practice of politics at that time was much different from the sophisticated process of money-raising and mud-slinging that it is now. People were more robust then and had the Yankee disposition of adhering tenaciously to their principles. Feelings ran high. Cider and rum flowed freely, and fisticuffs were not uncommon. Andrew Jackson's comments on his presidency are probably indicative of the tenor of the politics of that time. He is reported to have said that he had only two regrets: one, that he was

DEMOCRATIC REPUBLICAN TICKET.

EQUAL RIGHTS TO ALL.

THE SUPREMACY OF THE

CONSTITUTION AND CIVIL LAW.

THE ONLY GUARANTY OF PEACE AND PROSPERITY.

FOR GOVERNOR,

HIRAM R. ROBERTS.

For Railroad Commissioner,

Adams T. Peirce.

For Representative in Congress,

HENRY O. KENT.

For Councillor,

JEREMIAH BLODGETT.

For Senator,

JOSEPH D. WEEKS.

FRANKLIN EATON, Treasurer.
MARK PURMORT, Commissioner.
NATHANIEL W. CHENEY, Register.

unable to shoot Henry Clay, and two, that he could not hang his vice president, John C. Calhoun.

Reding reported on one town meeting that ran for three days. He reported that the Whigs and Free Soilers who opposed the Jackson Democrats resorted to rum and rowdyism to exclude the Democrats from voting. It became necessary for them to fight their way to the ballot box in order to cast their vote. At one time a fight went on in the hall that lasted nearly half an hour. The fact that the Whigs carried the election might have biased Reding's report.

The town history states that Reding was admirably trained. He served his newspaper apprenticeship under Isaac Hill of Portsmouth who owned the *New Hampshire Patriot* and who was well known for being outspoken. Both of them were uncompromising Democrats and strong supporters of Jackson, and there was never any doubt of their position on political matters. The old records are either missing or hard to locate, and I have not been able to find out just what he wrote, but during the 1830 elections Editor Reding published some things about Caleb that Caleb didn't like.

Although he won in the election, Caleb brought an action of libel against Reding in the next term of the Superior Court. It seems that it became an important case for it was tried four times. At that time the area was a hot bed for brilliant lawyers. Caleb and Reding each must have had the best. They managed to drag the case out for four years before a final decision was reached in 1835.

The final verdict was in favor of Caleb. I suppose that it was a victory of sorts, but it seems to have been a questionable one, and it was certainly not very profitable. Caleb was awarded damages assessed at one cent, which doesn't seem to speak very highly of the value of his reputation.

There is no record of Caleb or anyone else of my father's family messing around with politics after that. It  cannot be said that his political career ended up in a blaze of glory, and his experience may have discouraged those who came after him from having any ambition along that line. The generations of Eben and Ezra who followed Caleb and were prior to that of my father were content to be hillside farmers.

My father never seemed to take any interest even in local politics, but I think that he was purposely very devious about letting anyone know who he favored. I guess that he could be called a fence-straddler who tried to keep in the good graces of everyone. As I recall, he was able to get a tax rebate every year, no matter who was in office.

When I became interested enough to talk with him about the subject, I found out that his ideas about politicians were different from those that were held by my grandfather. He maintained that it was wrong to put so much blame on the politicians.

My father said that it is the people and not the politicians who are the ones responsible for the government. It is their vote that puts the politicians in office, and if they elect knotheads or horse thieves and log rollers they get what they deserve. He admitted that there could be occasions when the voters might be misled into electing undesirable people into office, which could be unfortunate. However, he pointed out that our system of government gives the voters plenty of chances for another crack at them, and they have the privilege of voting them out of office the next time around. My father made quite a point of the fact that the people are free to express their displeasure and dump practically the entire government every two years.

Ballot Box

WHS Collection

MOOSEHILLOCK FROM WARREN.

Forty Foot

mericans have always been a litigious bunch of people. The early Yankee's tendency for contention led to the Revolution, and the need for civil law arose almost as soon as the towns were settled. Most towns were some distance from the county courts where justice was dispensed. The early roads were atrocious, and many of the minor disputes were settled by the townspeople themselves.

A leading citizen was usually selected as a judge, and the jury was composed of the townspeople that were available. They were sitting in judgment on their neighbors and, even though the cases before them were minor, their deliberations must have been weighty and solemn. Some of the town histories that describe their early days tell of such hearings, and one account illustrates the diligence that was used in their deliberations.

Little's history of the town of Warren, New Hampshire, gives an account of a hearing in which one of the participants involved was a person whose first name was Moses. In reading the town history one gathers that he was sort of a character as he is mentioned in the record of other events that took place. It is easy to imagine that like many such individuals he was indispensable to the well-being of the town as he performed the menial tasks that others considered unworthy of their attention. One of his tasks might have been doing the general chores around the tavern for which he received his bed and fare and some access to the bar. Whatever the circumstances, he was evidently a frequent imbiber, and as a result he acquired a couple of characteristics for which he was well known. He had a congeniality that exuded good spirits and good cheer to everyone, and he possessed a bladder of generous capacity that had to be emptied frequently and often in a hurry.

Moses was a person of rather small stature and like many such people he tried to enhance it by telling tall stories of his exploits and experiences. His tales were so obviously farfetched that someone once remarked that they were not within forty feet of the truth, and he thereby became known around the countryside as "Forty Foot." The name was derisively descriptive of both his tall tales and his stature.

The other party involved in the hearing is nameless. The account describes him as a farmer from the hills who drove into town on one cold winter day for the purpose of trading and bartering for supplies at the general store, which was run by a Captain Merrill. His sleigh was an old-fashioned one with a high back and deep sides to keep the wind off of the driver. It was sort of a dilapidated vehicle which was once painted blue, and its back, which was about five feet high, had a crack near its top.

Warren, New Hampshire   Esther Whitcher Collection

The farmer hitched his horse and sleigh in the store shed while he was inside trading with Captain Merrill. His trading took some time, and at noon he went out to the shed to bait his horse and pick up his lunch, which his wife had wrapped in paper and placed on the seat of the sleigh. He found that someone had used the back of the sleigh as a splash board against which they had answered one of the calls of nature. The copious emission of fluid had entered through the crack and run down inside, soaking the farmer's lunch and rendering it unfit to eat.

The farmer was mad and vowed that he would have some sort of satisfaction. Naturally, the first suspect who came to mind was Forty Foot, and the farmer had him taken into custody on a charge of trespass. The account states that there was no judge present at the time, so a "reference" was appointed and they immediately proceeded with a hearing.

Forty Foot pled "not guilty," but he was tipsy, and most of those present at the hearing did not believe him. His condition and the general knowledge of the demands of his bladder made him the most likely suspect.

However, they were diligent in considering all aspects of the matter. The account of the hearing says that a two foot rule was procured and measurements were carefully made. Forty Foot's legs measured two feet and four inches from the floor to his crotch. The crack in the back of the sleigh was three feet six inches from the ground. After some deliberation the reference decided that Forty Foot did not have the necessary stature or pressure to have possibly done the deed, and he was acquitted. The account says that Forty Foot wept tears of joy over the result of the trial, and that the court, counsel, and spectators all took a smile at the bar of justice inside the store.

Warren, New Hampshire (1890's)

Rhubarbs

When the King and his council made their grants of land to those who expressed interest in founding and financing colonies in the New World, they did so with a lavish hand and a profound ignorance of the geography of the country. Controversy over them was bound to arise, and it took the King's Council between one hundred and one hundred and fifty years to settle the rhubarb. In 1620 the charter to the Plymouth Company granted them "that part of America lying between 40 and 48 degrees north latitude and in length by all the breadth aforesaid throughout the main land from sea to sea." That is quite a chunk of land!

In 1631 the Earl of Warwick granted and sold certain Lords and Gentlemen a strip of land 40 leagues in width that extended from Narragansett Bay to the South Sea which at that time was the Pacific Ocean. The grant was of land which he had evidently obtained from the Plymouth Company in 1630, and it became known as the Patent of Connecticut. The charter to the Massachusetts Bay colony also extended to the South Sea.

When the English took over the New Netherlands, King Charles gave his brother James, the Duke of York, a charter to the territory between the Connecticut and Delaware rivers, making the west bank of the Connecticut River New York's easterly boundary, and likewise causing controversy along boundaries with Pennsylvania, Delaware, and Maryland. There was so much land available that no attention was given to discrepancies that might create an overlap in the boundaries.

Both Connecticut and Massachusetts jumped the Connecticut River with settlements. When New York woke up to the fact that Connecticut was occupying

America Septentrionali

From septentrionales (literally the seven plow oxen),
the seven stars of the constellation Ursa Major
(Great Bear/Big Dipper), that point to the northern regions.

land that was within a short distance of the Hudson River, the two colonies almost went to war over the matter. The King's Council finally established a boundary line that ran northerly at a distance twenty miles east of the Hudson. It did not take long for Massachusetts to claim a northerly extension of the same line as its westerly boundary.

For years there was controversy between New Hampshire and Massachusetts over the line between them. The King's grant gave Massachusetts land that was bounded easterly by the Merrimack River and extended northerly to a point three miles north of it. In 1652 Governor Endicott commissioned Simon Willard and Edward Johnson to mark its northerly boundary. The surveyors chose a rock in the Winnipesaukee River at the outlet of that lake as Massachusetts' northeast corner and marked it with their initials and the name of Endicott. The rock was discovered in 1832 and is now a landmark in Endicott Park at Weirs Beach. Massachusetts claimed its northerly boundary to be a line that ran westerly from that point for an indefinite distance, and it granted townships within that area as far north as what is now Charlestown (old Number Four) on the Connecticut River.

In 1739 or 1740 the King's council ruled that Massachusetts' claim was considerably off base and that its northerly line was fifty miles or so to the south. New Hampshire gained a windfall of a large tract of land and about twenty-eight towns; a fact that might have been instrumental in convincing Benning Wentworth, who became its Royal Governor in 1741, that fishing in muddy waters could be profitable. According to the records of the New Hampshire Grants, he issued not less than 129 township charters within New York's boundaries until a King's order in council stopped him. Considering that he reserved 500 acres for himself in each township that he chartered, he ran a profitable operation.

New Hampshire itself was composed of grants made by the King to John Mason starting in 1621, the boundaries and ownership of which were in contention for almost 125 years until they were settled. One of Mason's grants gave him some sort of rights as far westerly as Lake Champlain.

The object of the above is to suggest that gobbling up land was probably a larger factor than freedom of worship in spurring the settlement of the New World, and to point out that descriptions of land which is being conveyed can be confusing and elusive as to boundaries, making them subject to controversy. It seems that the largest beneficiaries of England's stake in the New World were men who found favor with Kings and had visions of gaining control of large amounts of land to exploit. The discrepancies in the King's grants can be excused, for knowledge of the new country concerning its extent and its geographic features was very limited. Over the years as population increased and the land was split up into townships and lots and smaller parcels, the descriptive discrepancies increased; some of them through ignorance and laxity and some by deliberate Yankee manipulation.

For a large period of my life I was a land surveyor, working in the Connecticut Valley and northern New England. I became well acquainted with much of the land and its history and the instruments by which various parcels were conveyed. Most of my surveys, especially my early ones, were of so-called wild land; land that was heavily forested and unsuited for either cultivation or habitation. A lot of it had once been occupied by early settlers and abandoned for greener pastures. It had usually been logged over two or three times; the old corners and lines had been obliterated and changed by trespassers, and some of the land had literally been stolen.

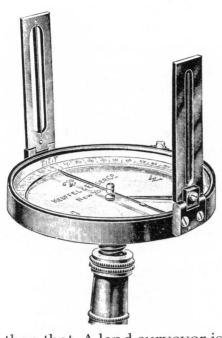

Field Compass

The author's compass was obtained from Charlie Roby, who drove the Nulhegan for Van Dyke. It has run many miles of line. *(From A Manual for Northern Woodsmen, Austin Cary, 1915).*

One definition describes surveying as the angular and lineal measurement of land, which is relatively simple, but there is much more to it than that. A land surveyor is supposed to travel in the footsteps of the one who made the original survey, which might have been done a century or more before. Those footsteps were a pretty dim trail to follow, and changes that had occurred over the years and some of the deed descriptions made following them a difficult task.

From the beginning, when land began to be divided and transferred, deeds were made out by laymen who were usually Justices of the Peace. They depended upon the parties involved for a description of what was being conveyed. The descriptions may have been plain to the parties participating in the deal at that time, but they often became Greek to later generations, and the task of unraveling them became the first priority of the land surveyor. The Justices often added to the confusion by becoming so obsessed with using flowery language that they sometimes negated the description itself. There are many deeds of land today that refer back to those old muddy descriptions, and there are even town lines that are difficult to determine or to follow. Some are still a subject of controversy.

It used to be the custom for the selectmen of adjoining towns to get together to perambulate their town lines every few years with the object of keeping them well marked. However, according to some reports, the procedure was often regarded as an outing and was done with the aid of a jug. As a result there are some awfully wide town lines in existence today.

Some of the deed descriptions are doozies, like one I encountered when I was engaged to do a survey of land by a person who had received a deed in payment of some obligation. He had no idea of where the land was located, except that it was in Haverhill, and after chasing deeds back for over fifty years to find its description, I was no more enlightened than he was. The first and only description I found was in a sheriff's tax deed which deeded "a piece of land east of Woodsville." Woodsville is a New Hampshire village located on the Connecticut River, which is the western boundary of the town of Haverhill. The east and west breadth of the town is approximately six miles, and it contains an awful lot of land east of Woodsville.

Another description of land that I encountered in a survey deeded a person named Tewksbury "the land which I showed him yesterday." Try following those footsteps. There are many descriptions almost as vague and confusing, and a survey usually became a royal headache. For years land was conveyed by deeds that referred only to the deed preceding it, and tracing those deeds back to the one which contained the original description was like descending a long series of steps through a dungeon in search of some light at its end. When one did find a description that might contain metes and bounds, its starting point could be the corner of some ancient farm barnyard that had disappeared in forest growth many years previously. Sometimes one searched through deeds until he ran into a dead end and could go no further; an indication that the land was probably stolen. It has been done.

The vagaries concerning land are interesting. There have been times when people shun it due to excessive taxation or times of severe stress such as the Depression of the 1930's. During the Depression certain types of land were a drug on the market. They were a burden, and there were people who were land poor. There was a long stretch of years when land transactions were inactive, rendering dealings subject to sharp practices. There were a few people in the north country who were notorious for their shady dealings and whenever a surveyor found them in the line of deeds he was researching he could prepare for trouble.

Those old Yankee traders who were resourceful in gaining an edge for themselves contributed to the confusion. At times they did so by misstating the acreage involved in a deed. One tract of land with a vague description that called for fifteen acres turned out to contain over eighty acres when it was properly surveyed. There was a period during which land was taxed according to the acreage stated in the deeds, and the idea was to own eighty acres and be taxed for fifteen. It was a ploy that eventually became apparent, and the towns took steps to remedy their tax lists.

This practice of owning land without paying taxes on it is being done today. Some people, operating under the guise of non-profit and tax-free institutions such as private schools or religious organizations, may be getting away with it.

In addition, overstatement of acreage was practiced with the intent to deceive. For several decades after the Civil War a number of people abandoned their farms and went west. The abandoned land eventually became cheap enough so that it attracted speculation. I have found numerous tracts that appear to have been purchased for that purpose, and when they were resold the acreage was greatly exaggerated. When the land is surveyed the true acreage may be as much as fifty percent less than the deed calls for. The overstatement or understatement of acreage became so widespread that acreage has become the least important call in a deed, and a surveyor is usually blamed and chastised severely when his survey results in less acreage than that called for in the deed.

In fact, a surveyor is a *persona non grata* more often than he is appreciated, even by those who hire him. I once did a survey to settle a rhubarb over some rhubarb. It involved two adjoining town lots and the owners,  a man and a woman, were at each other's throats over the ownership of a patch of rhubarb which was around their back corner. Each claimed ownership, and was trying to prevent the other from picking any of it. When the lots were surveyed according to the deeds, it turned out that neither of them owned it. The rhubarb actually belonged to a person who lived on the next street and the three lots had a back line in common.

Those two who had been fighting over the patch joined forces and jumped down my throat. The incident brought to mind a comment of one of my early mentors when I first expressed an interest in practicing land surveying. He said that any person considering being a surveyor had to have a thick skin and a weak mind.

Today a large portion of the most viable wild land has been surveyed, and much of it divided into lots for development. A lot of perimeter surveys have been made, and the headaches concerning them have been ironed out. The accent today seems to be on meticulous accuracy of measurement instead of having to meet the necessity of providing a judge with proofs in black and white by deeds that have been recorded; proofs that one has really traveled in the footsteps of the old original surveyors and found evidence of their work on the ground.

Cruiser's and Logger's Blaze

The author's blaze was a mitten made by hanging two blazes on a tree in a prominent way.

Surveyors' Marks

These were formed by initials scribed on boundary lines and at corners. They were usually very unobtrusive. WK was for "Will Keniston" and that below is the author's.

Walls

If you do much off-trail hiking in the heavily wooded and isolated hills of New England, especially in New Hampshire or Vermont, you will come upon remnants of former habitation. Some of them may date back two hundred years or more to the first settlement of the land, and are a part of its history. The most readily discernible objects are stone walls. Many of them are buried in the debris of the years with only a portion of them visible. A few may be completely buried, and their presence can be recognized only by a practiced eye.

Those walls were not built haphazardly or without reason. An inspection of many of them will show that the stones are carefully laid with a precision and a pride of workmanship that often seems to be lacking in today's society. Many of them extend for long distances, running in a straight line over hill and dale and often up mountain sides. Such long walls are usually an indication of the location of one of the range lines which were run to divide the tiers of lots when a town was first lotted at its inception many years ago.

Except for the river bottoms, a large part of New England is composed of rough and stony hillsides. After the land had been cleared of its trees, a settler in such places was faced with the disposal of a large crop of stones which had to be removed before the land could be properly worked. What better place could be found to put them than on a boundary line where they would serve for years to come as sentinels of a man's domain? Many of the walls were built by men who did nothing else. I once saw an old contract of indenture in which a man was hired to build stone walls. His pay was bed and fare with an allowance of tobacco and rum and three dollars a month, hard money.

One can happen upon other traces of habitation which are not as readily discernible as the stone walls. Close inspection of an isolated pile of stones may reveal that they were once a chimney of a fire pit or a fireplace which formed practically the entire end wall of a small, crude, one room shelter. A little digging may bring forth shards of old metal and charcoal, and often the outlines and the foundation stones of the shelter itself can be traced.

When a man who had trod through a wilderness toting an axe and a gun, and possibly a blanket and a kettle, located the land he had purchased or which had been allotted to him in some remote township, he didn't waste any time putting his mark on it. The minute he crossed the line into his domain he made his pitch. He did so by putting up a small, crude, one room shelter which he occupied while making the first clearing of the land, and which told the world that he had taken possession. Even in those days there was plenty of mischief concerning land, and possession was considered to be nine points of the law.

The chicanery began with the land speculators who made an early appearance. The only people who knew the land were the Indians and a few transients. As a rule, the Indians merely traveled through it, stopping at different places to plant or to fish and hunt, and then moving on. The first settlers were preceded only by them, and an occasional hunter or trapper, and those who surveyed the land. The surveyors had to be the first ones that made any lasting mark on the wilderness.

The Royal Governor of New Hampshire, Benning Wentworth, from whom all blessings flowed at that time, could not very well make a grant of a township to its proprietors whom he was milking without having

Royal Governor Benning Wentworth
N.H. Hist. Society #F3426

enough of a survey made so that he could give a reasonably good description of it. Furthermore, he reserved 500 acres for himself out of each town that he granted, and he made certain that they were well monumented and marked on the ground by the surveyors.

After Wentworth had exacted his toll, it became the speculators' turn to wring whatever gain they could out of the land. They did so under the guise of proprietors, and it is safe to say that ninety-five percent of them were never within a hundred miles of the land which they were peddling. The agents who represented them were not averse to selling a piece of hillside twice or to moving corners, and a man needed to show strong evidence of occupation and a willingness to fight for what he claimed was his. Skullduggery was quite rife in both high and low places.

As it has been since the beginning of time, those who were well placed and drew the longest bow got the cream. In those days, as far as the land was concerned, the cream was the fertile river bottoms and its terraces. The unfortunate land-hungry settlers were forced to wage their battle with the stony and unproductive hillsides. They put up their shelters, cleared the land of its trees and stones, and labored to wring an existence from the stubborn soil. It must have been a backbreaking and frustrating task; so much so that many of them abandoned their clearings at the first rumors of more viable country elsewhere.

The land which they labored so hard to settle and to clear and cultivate quickly reverted to a wilderness, which obliterated all but a few marks of their occupation. There are remains of entire settlements which once had subsistence homesteads and small water-powered mills to serve them, that are hidden away in remote valleys and hollows which are now heavily forested. Except perhaps for a name, which is only a part of local lore, they are forgotten and unknown. The only things left to show that they were once occupied are the stone walls that were built and the foundations of crude shelters and a few isolated cellar holes; mute evidence of a hard-scrabble existence.

One can even find well-populated cemeteries under the forest canopy. The cellar holes are filled with debris, and many have trees growing out of them which are over a foot in diameter. Some still have shrubbery and flowers growing around them, indicating that the place was once a home — a lilac bush or morning

glories, and a sprinkling of other flowers, which are the progeny of ones that were probably planted by some lonely woman many years ago.

To a land surveyor working in such isolated areas scores of years after their abandonment, trying to reconstruct the jig saw puzzle of the old land holdings, all of those ancient evidences of occupation are grist for his mill. Often they can speak quite eloquently, and on one occasion, early in my surveying practice, a voice from a grave rescued me from what could have been a damaging lawsuit. The controversy was over a survey which I had made, and it claimed that a line that I had run and designated as a Range Line was in error. A substantial amount of land was involved. My reputation and credibility were also at stake, and I began a much more thorough deed search than I had previously done.

One of the lots in my survey had been settled by a man named Solomon Hunt. He deeded it to another party around 1820, and in his deed he reserved a plot of land for his grave, said plot being "a piece of land one rod square, adjacent to the Range Line."

Needless to say, I began a foot by foot search of my line. I found old Solomon's grave. It was enclosed on each side by walls which were covered by debris. Their tops were barely visible, and my line was within a foot or so of the grave site. I uncovered his marker, that was nothing more than a slab on which the letters S H could be traced. I bared my head and paid him homage. Those few words which he had put into his deed and the walls around his grave that had been built over one hundred years previously, upheld my line and negated any lawsuit.

If you are the sort of person who likes to travel untrammeled areas, and you encounter an old piece of wall or something unusual all by its lonesome in some wild, isolated spot, observe it with respect. It may have a story to tell.

Country
Years

Introduction to Country Years

Lots of old-timers tell stories. Very few of them, however, ever write them down. That's probably because they don't realize how thoroughly defunct is the American oral tradition. And rare indeed is the old-timer who writes his reminiscences with such a mix of wit, humor, and clarity as Bill Morse.

His genius, as with any storyteller, lies in the details. He recalls, for example, the itchy torment of a wool union suit during spells of warm weather; the aroma of a sack of asafetida hung round the neck to ward off illness; and the specific alcohol content of popular medicines that achieved popularity during Prohibition. His innocent delight is often infectious, as when he describes the effects of sulphur and molasses on a schoolroom or a church full of kids in springtime.

Bill's paean to old-fashioned baked pork and beans is enough to make you rush right out and buy a bean pot. Beans are baked traditionally on Saturday afternoon, he points out, because the Puritans believed it a sin to cook on the Sabbath. They got through it with their beans and, as Bill suggests, a little humor, besides.

This is not a Currier & Ives portrait of life three-quarters of a century ago. Bill's trains scatter soot and ashes wherever they go; his garrulous party-line neighbors are exasperating; and he remembers the Depression as truly frightening for many people. Still, there is rare beauty in his recollections — the midnight express and "...the echo of the long, loon-like wail of the whistle bouncing off the hills of the valley." There are interesting features of a culture almost forgotten — "...one who smoked cigarettes was considered to be a sissy!"

Most of all, there is a long, loving look back at the hard country and the even harder times that made Bill and his generation the tough cookies that they were. "No one became affluent in his activities," he remembers, "but the struggle to make ends meet seemed as beneficial to a person's well-being as the pittance which he earned."

Will Lange
Etna, New Hampshire

(Willem Lange resides in Etna, N.H., and is a master storyteller in his own right. He is the author of *Tales From the Edge of the Woods*, University Press of New England, 1998.)

Materiel Medica

Medical knowledge, as we know it today, was not very advanced in the early years of the 1900's. People related many of their health problems of that time to the vagaries of the seasons, and they used a lot of old time home remedies that had been handed down over the years. Some of them were bizarre; many of them were vile; and a few of them might have been beneficial.

Winter was the season that seemed to call for the most effort to prevent illness. Preventive measures were taken at the first onset of cold weather. We donned our winter underwear of heavy woolen union suits, which were one piece outfits with what was called a barn door seat. We lived and slept in them. At our house my mother provided us with clean ones every Saturday night when we had our bath, but a lot of other households were not as picky. Once they had donned their winter underwear, there were people who did not shed it until spring. They could get pretty ripe. If the wind was right, you could tell who was coming down the road before they made their appearance. Whenever we had a thaw and the weather became warm, those woolen union suits became itchy and very uncomfortable. In addition to union suits some people wore an old stocking around their neck all winter. I had a cousin who was brought up to do so. He had a long neck, and with the stocking around it he resembled a ring-necked pheasant.

My mother started her winter ritual by setting a small kettle or sauce pan — I think that it was cast iron — on one of the back lids of the kitchen stove. She kept several onions simmering in it throughout the winter.

She added maple sugar or honey to them, and the mixture became a gelatinous mass which was doled out to us by the spoonful at the first sign of a scratchy throat. It was not a bad tasting concoction, and it did soothe a sore throat. It seems that onions were considered to have some therapeutic value in those days. When my father had pneumonia, the doctor had us round up a lot of onions. We had two nurses who gave my father around the clock care, and the doctor had them boil the onions and fill pillow cases with them. They kept my father's chest covered with those hot onions while he was sick. I do not know if they were of any value or not, but he recovered.

Hot cider and ginger before going to bed was a popular cold remedy which was effective in easing the misery of a cold, and at times it really seemed to cure one. A chest cold called for a mustard plaster. I think that they could be purchased at the store, but my mother made the ones she used on us. She mixed mustard with some sort of grease or oil that was mentholated, smeared it on a piece of cloth, warmed it up, and slapped it on our chests before we went to bed. The vilest tasting stuff that I remember taking as a cold preventative was cod liver oil, which was sometimes touted as a touch of sunshine. A spoonful of that tasted so bad that it was hard to swallow and keep down.

Other external remedies that I can recall were used for cuts and bruises. Small cuts and abrasions were often treated with the resin that was obtained by puncturing the blisters that were on the trunks of balsam fir. There was always a small tin of it around the house which we had collected. Larger cuts that were not quite worthy of a doctor's attention were treated by bandaging them with a piece of salt pork. The kids went barefoot all summer, and between nails and barbed wire and other sharp objects their feet took a lot of punishment. A knotted rag that held some salt pork on one's foot was a

badge worthy of some attention. If there was danger of infection, a well-worked gob of chewing tobacco was often slapped on the cut. All such remedies seemed to be very effective at healing.

Some of the doctors had their special remedies. One doctor from around Boston who spent the hunting seasons with us used to send up one or two of his patients every spring during sugaring season. They had tuberculosis which was quite prevalent at that time. His instructions were for them to spend all of their time at the sugar house whenever we were boiling. During a boiling session a sugar house becomes filled with steam, the vapor of which is saturated with the sweet and heavy aroma of boiling sap. I suppose that the doctor's theory was that the inhalation of the vapor was beneficial to his patients. They were usually a nuisance to us, but his patients provided some small income during a dull season.

During the First World War the influenza epidemic hit the country. It was a devastating disaster that resulted in many deaths. Our area was not immune to it. My mother was the only one in our family who contracted it. Doctors and nurses had more than they could take care of, and most people had to depend upon their own resources for care.

My father took care of my mother, and he never entered her room without first taking a drink of whiskey and a big chew of tobacco. My mother recovered, and my father's preventive precautions were evidently effective for he escaped contracting the flu.

My grandfather was sort of a herbalist who believed in the effectiveness of some herbs. The only thing in that line that he introduced me to was the use of boiled sweet fern as a poultice for poison ivy. It was effective. He cooked up other concoctions that were revolting. He had one that he made by boiling the inner bark of poplar that he claimed was a stomach conditioner. I tried taking a spoonful of it once, and had to throw up. Any stomach that could stand that didn't need conditioning.

Real elderly people were addicted to wearing a small bag filled with asafetida which they hung from their necks as a sort of amulet to ward off sickness. It had an extremely fetid and penetrating stench that was offensive enough to ward off anything. The odor from one small bag was enough to permeate an entire house. A dead skunk around the premises would be preferable. One of the meanest tricks a kid could play on a teacher was to smuggle some asafetida into the schoolroom and hide it. Finding it took priority over all school work. If the teacher discovered the one who was responsible for the prank, she wielded the old hardwood ruler, and he could be sure of having some ungodly sore knuckles for a few days.

When spring began to roll around, there was no need to use asafetida bags to perfume the schoolroom. The sulphur and molasses that we were dosed with did the trick. The mixture was a spring tonic that was supposed to purify one's blood of its winter accumulations of impurities. If the odor of the gas that resulted from its ingestion was any indication, it was successful in doing so. The mixture was fed to the kids by the spoonful for three weeks or so, and the discharge of gas which it generated provided a distinctive atmosphere around the school room or any other place. It was particularly noticeable at church services as the windows of the church were rarely opened. A few resourceful boys tanked up with sulphur and molasses could add a lot of spice to a dry Sunday sermon. The best part of it was that no one kid could be singled out to be punished for fouling the atmosphere for it could be done quietly and was a natural phenomenon.

Most of the home remedies were used to prevent or treat minor ills such as colds or sore throats or cuts that were not life threatening. Our elders treated the more serious disorders of the body with the so-called patent medicines that were sold in great quantities. There were medicines guaranteed to cure any ailment known to either men or women. They were widely advertised in all of the newspapers and magazines, and I suppose that those ads were the forerunners of the ones that television beams to the world today.

Some of the medicines were popular enough to become household words, and were used until the middle of the century. The ones that I particularly remember being dosed with as a kid were Father John's, Syrup of Figs, Castoria, and the old standby, castor oil.

Cloverilla
Bath, New Hampshire

Father John's Elixir   Blaisdell Collection

Some of them may be used today. Most of the patent medicines that were sold to the older people contained a high enough percentage of alcohol to make them feel better in short order. Temperance workers or church deacons could dose themselves with those without being branded as backsliders. There are reports of some medicines that ran as high as forty-eight percent alcohol, and at the start of Prohibition in 1920 there was a big demand for them — so much so that the federal agents began to crack down on some of them. From 1930 until 1955 we had many logging camps in operation, and next to tobacco the patent medicines were the biggest sellers in the wangans.

If a jobber didn't make any money on his logging contract, the sales of patent medicines alone allowed him to show a profit on his wangan account. Troutman's Cough Syrup was one of the biggest sellers, regardless of the season, winter or summer. I would guess that it was at least one-third alcohol, and we used to buy it by the gross.

The medicines were blatantly advertised in most of the newspapers and magazines of the day, and those ads offer a fine example of the pitchman's art. They were very suggestive, and were not the least bit reticent in describing the symptoms and the afflictions which they claimed to cure. Old-timers called such medicines Snake Oil or Kickapoo Juice.

Gerald Carson wrote a well-illustrated book about patent medicines that was titled *One For a Man, Two For a Horse.* I cannot recall any specific medicine making that claim, but almost anything was possible at that time.

There was one patent medicine that was sold as a pain killer — I think its name was Davis' Pain Killer. Its ads stressed the fact that it could be used either externally or internally. It is reported that Davis' Pain Killer became an important ingredient in a thermometer allegedly devised by Jack McQuesten, a trader on the Yukon during the Klondike gold rush days. The thermometer was made up of four vials in a rack. One contained quicksilver which was the first to freeze. The second and third vials contained whiskey and kerosene which next froze in that order. The fourth vial contained Davis' Pain Killer which was the last to freeze. When that began to gel, about all that a man could do to prevent freezing was to nurse a bottle of it while burying himself in the blankets on his bunk.

Sears Roebuck, who did not intend to be outdone by anyone, had their own brand of medicines which they sold through their catalogue. Their drug section took up about twenty pages, and a perusal of it can be quite enlightening. One can encounter things that put our present drug industry with all of its extravagant claims to shame. The edition of the Sears catalogue

No. 111 has a twenty minute cold cure which is described as being sufficient to stop a cold and prevent it from getting any further. One could buy a bottle of Blackberry Balsam that was described as "a pleasant and effective remedy for Dysentery, Diarrhoea, Looseness, Asiatic Cholera, Cholera Morbus, Summer Complaint, Cholera Infantum, Colic, Cramps, Griping Pains, Sour Stomach, Sick and Nervous Headache, Pain or Sickness of the Stomach, Vomiting, Restlessness and Inability to Sleep, Wind in the Stomach and Bowels, Hysterics and for all bowel affections."

An entire page was devoted to its Vin Vitae which was described not as a medicine or a stimulant, but a tonic which made women strong and built up undeveloped and puny children. There are medicines listed which discourage the tobacco habit and cures those who are addicted to the use of liquor. One is uncertain whether to laugh at the descriptions and their guarantees of cures or to marvel at them.

Molière, a writer of the seventeenth century, is credited with the saying, "Nearly all men die of their remedies and not of their illnesses." Thanks to the medical advances that have been made, that is not as true now as it was then. However, the hype has not changed much from that which was used to push the patent medicines of the early years of the century. One does not have to look far through the magazines or watch much television before becoming aware that we are being bombarded with ads that closely resemble those of the pitchmen who touted the patent medicines of the bygone days. Our gullibility is probably as great as that of the people who purchased the panaceas that were advertised a century or more ago.

City

The comedian, W. C. Fields, had a line that he was fond of using quite often. It concerned elephants and women. He said that they were nice to look at, but that he wouldn't want to own one. I do not know if he coined the phrase or if he stole it from someone. I mention it because in a way it expresses my feelings concerning large cities. They are nice places to visit occasionally, but I decided that I did not care about living in one.

Boston was the only large city that I became well acquainted with during my lifetime. I was exposed to it at an early age. My grandfather had a brother, known to us as Uncle George, who lived in the outskirts of the city, and I visited him numerous times when I was a kid. My aunt and uncle did not have any children, and they entertained me royally. They had lived in Medford for years. My uncle was a font of information on the history of the city, and he introduced me to the historical places of old Boston and also to the more modern developments that had replaced some of the old city; places that were modern at that time, which was during the decade before 1920. He was sort of a living guide book to the city, and I became fairly well steeped in its early history.

A visit to the big city of Boston, which was often called the Hub, was an event of some consequence. It involved a train ride of several hours, and the few people in our area who had made it and spent some time in the city acquired an aura of distinction and were considered to be well traveled.

The first trip that is impressed upon my memory occurred probably when I was about nine or ten years of age around 1913. I was in knee breeches. It was a red-letter event, for my parents decided that I was old enough to make the trip alone if someone would meet me when I arrived at North Station. We lived about one hundred and fifty miles north of Boston, and it meant a train ride of around four hours. During the first two decades of the century the train was the only practical way to make a trip of any length. A long trip could be both exciting and tedious.

A visit to the city and its many attractions was a thrilling experience to a kid who had only been used to the rural life of the boondocks. My first excursion to Revere Beach with its roller coaster rides and its bright lights and amusement parlors was like a trip to the land of Oz. As I recall, it started with a ferry ride from either Rowes Wharf or Lewis Wharf across the harbor to East Boston where we took a train to the beach. The glamour of the lights and the attractions was overwhelming.

After the First World War my grandfather sold his creamery to H. P. Hood, and one of his sons was included in the deal. As a result I had a second uncle to visit who also lived in Medford. He was a motorcycle enthusiast. He had a large Indian with a side car. He enjoyed making it hum, and he was a lot of fun.

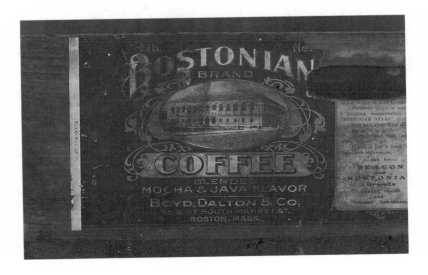

He had an early morning milk route in Charlestown. When I visited him, my cousin and I used to get
up before 4 o'clock and help with his route so that he
could finish work early, and give us more time to ride
around the countryside during the day. I still have a
vivid recollection of those early morning hours delivering milk to the many apartment houses and the echo
of our horse's hooves as he traveled over the cobble-
stones. Most of our excursions on the motorcycle were
along the North Shore and Cape Ann. We often ended
up digging clams at Ipswich or Rowley, and bringing
home a bag of steamers.

FANEUIL HALL.

My visits to both uncles were usually of short
duration, but they were busy ones, and by the time I
was twenty I had experienced a good introduction to
Boston and some of its environs. It was natural for me
to gravitate to the place upon the completion of my
education. I became employed in the city as an accoun-

tant. I found out that living and working there was not as enjoyable as the short visits that I had previously made to my uncles. I abhorred being chained indoors to a desk, and living like a pigeon in a pigeon hole. I was like the tobacco-chewing farmer who expressed a dislike for the city, complaining that he felt penned in, and that there was no place to spit. I did not look forward to having my life ruled by columns of figures, and I became homesick for the open country and the hills. It took about a couple of years for me to conclude that I was not meant for city life. I folded my tent and returned home to the farm and the woods. The Depression soon began to appear, and during its early years I visited the city occasionally, and became thankful that I had escaped the troubles that many were experiencing.

The Boston that I knew was the one of the Prohibition and the early Depression years, during the 1920's and the early 1930's. Neither decade was very nice. There was a book published about the city of that period titled *Bawdy Boston*. As I recall, it caused quite a stir. I did not return to the city for an extended visit until some fifty years later, and except for a few spots, I had to learn my way around the place again. Copley Place was in the process of construction, and I got lost there.

Scollay Square had disappeared entirely. According to its history, Scollay Square was part of the early settlement, and became the crossroads of the city. Later, before and during my time, it reigned for years as the bawdy spot of Boston, well known to sailors in every port throughout the world for its many amusement attractions. The Old Howard Theater with the bumps and grinds and the striptease acts of its burlesque queens headed all of its other attractions — the penny arcades, the shooting galleries, the peep shows, the tattoo parlors, and the speakeasies. The only thing left of the square now that is recognizable is the old steaming tea kettle which was originally the sign of a tea house. According to the guidebooks some homage has been paid to what it was best known for.

The location of the Old Howard stage is marked by a circular plaque. To the rustic bumpkins from the boondocks a trip to the city without a visit to Scollay Square and the Old Howard was a non-event.

The sea-going atmosphere of the wharves along Atlantic Avenue is a thing of the past. Instead of providing berths for ocean-going freighters and occasionally a liner, the wharves have been converted into luxurious apartments, office buildings, restaurants and museums.

The freighters that used to line the wharves have given way to pleasure boats, and the romance of the sea seems to have departed.

There are other changes too numerous to mention. Like the change in Scollay Square which replaces the seedy old blocks that housed its bawdy attractions, the renovations have made the city more attractive, and to many people a nice and interesting place to visit.

Beans

"Beans, beans, a wonderful fruit —
The more you eat, the more you toot!"

The kids of my time got a kick out of reciting that ditty. Beans were a staple of our diet in the early decades of the century. Every Saturday my mother baked a pot of them. Her bean pot was a large one — it must have held at least four quarts. We had beans hot out of the oven for supper every Saturday night, and there was enough left over to provide us with lunches throughout the next week. By the following Saturday the pot would be empty and ready for another day in the oven. Those beans had a toot in them, and everyone tooted all over the place. No one was immune to their effect. A good bean toot could not be avoided. It was a sort of hiccup in reverse. Sometime around the middle of the century, agricultural scientists discovered some way to grow a bean without a toot, and I guess that by now most of the beans are tootless — at least the New England varieties seem to be.

The bean is entitled to a lot of praise. An old Indian legend relates that a crow brought them a kernel of corn in one ear and a bean in the other from the field of one of their Gods. The Indians cultivated them, and they were here when the Pilgrims arrived. One of the first things the Pilgrims did when they landed in the New World was to plunder an Indian cache of its corn and a bag of beans. They were resourceful in their reasoning. Instead of calling it plunder, they labeled it as a gift from God. The corn and the beans provided by the Indians helped the newcomers to survive their first winter. The Pilgrims learned the Indian way to plant and cook them, and for a while they were dependent on them as staple foods. The Indians buried the beans in underground pits to cook slowly, wrapping them in deer hides with maple sugar and bear fat. The early settlers adopted and improved the process, and the old bean pots and baked beans have been a New England institution ever since. Even the Boston Brahmins ate them, making Boston Baked Beans a household name, and those high and mighty ones must have tooted. The early Boston baseball team became known as the Bean Eaters.

Beans became glamorous things to us in my boyhood when the log drive came down the river in late spring. Until 1915 long logs were driven down the Connecticut River, and when the wangans — the cook tents and other camping equipment — made their overnight bivouacs, many of the local people would flock to the spot for a meal of beans. Our farm was about ten miles from the river, and I can remember a couple of occasions when we went over and watched the drive

Crew boat for men and supplies   N.H. Hist. Society #F4560
during the log drives on the Connecticut River

and ate at the camp. The wangans would travel ahead
of the drive and set up at a spot where the men could
be bunked and fed at the end of the day. The site was
usually some meadow, and the evening meal was pork
and beans and hot biscuits served in great quantities,
along with thick ginger and molasses cookies as large as
saucers. The pork and beans were baked in huge iron
kettles that were buried in the ground where they
cooked all day, and were known as "bean hole beans."
They were good!

Part of the wangan and some of the men were
usually held for several days near McIndoes while the
logs were put through the rapids known as Mulliken's
Pitch and those known as the Narrows at Woodsville.
The drive's first overnight stop below Woodsville was
in our area, and it drew an audience. That part of the
river that ran through our countryside was pretty tame
water, and the drive through it did not offer much excitement. The bean hole beans and the biscuits were the

big attraction. The local people who came around for a meal seemed to be welcome, and it must have been quite an expense to the drive to feed them. The cooks fed everyone who showed up. I suspect that doing so was probably a public relations policy, as a lot of the farmers and people who lived on the river considered the drive to be a nuisance. It was not considered at all as glamorous as it was later purported to be. A heavy rain and high water could leave logs stranded on the meadows and raise hob with a farmer. Bean hole beans and biscuits could act as sort of a leaven to them.

Baked beans have been a staple food to loggers ever since the first camp was built. Writers of the history of the early camps say that a bean hole pit was dug in one corner of the camp for the purpose of cooking pork and beans. They must have been preferable to any food that was cooked in an open kettle which was suspended from a tripod and hung over a fire. Wormy meat, flies, and any other foreign objects that found their way into the kettle must have taken second place to good old pork and beans that had been buried in the ground to cook. In the logging camps of my time baked beans had their place on the table morning, noon, and night. We bought beans in hundred-pound bags. A large camp would go through a bag of beans in a couple of days.

Reports of the old-time farmer-drovers who loaded their produce into pungs in the winter and teamed the long trips to the city markets say that they carried frozen bean porridge with them for their food. They stopped overnight at the taverns to stable and bait their horses and drive the cold from their bones with hot grog, but they preferred their beans to the tavern fare.

Baked beans are one of our ancestors' staple foods that have endured to the present time. Most of those that are consumed today come from a can, and there are many people who are not acquainted with them in any

other form. There are a few diehards who take the trouble of preparing them the old-fashioned way by letting them bake in the oven all day, and there may be some who still follow the ritual of having them for their Saturday night meal; a ritual that purportedly originated with the Puritans to keep them from sin. They led their lives in accordance with the concepts of the Bible, and the fourth commandment says that there shall be no work done on the Sabbath. The Puritans took those commandments literally. By baking beans on Saturday the Puritans were able to eat on Sunday without committing the sin of cooking on their day of worship.

The canned beans that grace the shelves of today's supermarkets are well suited to the hit and run tempo of today's life. Although they are a poor substitute for the home cooked product, a case can be made for them. During my logging years we would sometimes spend one or two nights in the woods when we were cruising a large tract in some wilderness area.

Canned beans, bacon, bread and coffee were our diet. A half dozen cans of beans, a slab of bacon, with a couple loaves of bread and some coffee do not take up much room; they are light in weight and easily prepared. All one needs is a knife, a can opener, and a fry pan, and in short order he can have a meal that will stand by him an entire day.

However, the tin can cannot compete with the old-fashioned bean pot. Removing the cover from a pot of savory pork and beans that has spent the day slowly simmering in an oven is a lot different from opening a tin can and heating its contents over some coals or in a frypan. The canned beans are handy at times and some of them are fairly good, but compared to the real thing, they are not what they are "tooted" to be.

Blacksmith

Longfellow, in his poem of the village smithy, paid homage to the blacksmith with his large and sinewy hands, but he did not offer any description of the shop itself. Even in his day, blacksmith shops probably were such cluttered messes that no one could wax very poetic about them. Years later, in the early decades of the nineteen hundreds when I was a youngster on the scene, the blacksmith shops that served communities dependent on a farm economy had such a disorderly appearance that they could be called the forerunners of our present day junk yards.

The shop in our small village was no exception. It was surrounded by a tangled mass of old worn out farm implements waiting for repairs or for the salvage of their metal parts — old plow points, harrows, sled runners, wagon wheels, broken down hayrakes, cultivators and buggies — and by all sorts of scrap metal. The only open place around it was the doorway. The interior

of the shop was a hovel of semi-darkness. Its grimy, cobwebby windows did not let in much light.

The glowing coals of the forge and the bright colored spray of sparks radiating from horse shoes as the smith pounded them into shape on the anvil made the shop resemble a witches' dungeon. Piles of old horse shoes and hoof shavings surrounded the forge on which hung a dozen or so large tongs, hammers, and other tools of the trade. A couple of anvils and a wooden tub of water occupied the space beside the forge, and there was a timbered frame with slings on it that was used to hold oxen and unruly horses while they were being shod.

Kegs of horse shoes, chain links, and shelves with boxes of bolts, shoe caulks, and nails lined the walls. There were but few spots that were vacant. The walls and everything in the shop were covered with an accumulation of soot and grime, and the place had an aroma that is difficult to describe unless one is familiar with the smell of hot iron just out of the forge, of singed horses' hooves, or of horse manure mixed with the smell of coal dust and cinders. The aroma was distinctive and surprisingly not at all unpleasant when one became used to it.

The shop that served our countryside was located down in the village, and the blacksmith played an important role in our farm economy. In addition to shoeing horses, which is an art unto itself, he was adept at repairing broken and worn-out farm equipment, keeping it going long after it was ready to give up the ghost. I became well acquainted with the blacksmith and his workplace, and they are among the earliest of my childhood memories.

My father's logging and farming activities required the use of a number of horses, and when I was a little shaver I often accompanied him when he took them to the shop to be shod. When I was old enough to drive a pair of horses, my father sometimes gave me the chore of driving them down to the shop to have the job done, and I naturally gravitated to the place whenever I found myself in the village with time on my hands. It was a good place to hang out and keep out of trouble.

The shop was busy, and there were usually one or more farmers waiting to have their horses shod. One learned about their troubles, and picked up the gossip of the countryside. The activities of the widow and whoever happened to be seeing her currently were discussed. Whatever a young lad learned in listening to the gossip was usually newsworthy and educational.

There were times when events made the shop an exciting place. The blacksmith was not a particularly large person, but like Longfellow's smith he was strong and sinewy. A fringe of hair that was a mixture of red and gray surrounded a bald spot on top of his head,

Some Early Blacksmith Tools

Blacksmith Chaps

Right – Buttress for paring a hoof
before fitting a horseshoe
Below – Horse mouth speculum
to allow a good look inside

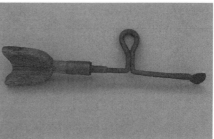

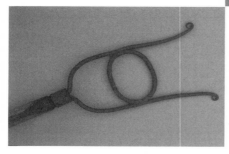

Edwin Blaisdell Collection
North Haverhill, New Hampshire

and he wore glasses. His uniform was a leather apron. He had a quick temper, and could swear fluently when provoked. I had picked up a few swear words while hanging around my father's loggers, but they were low on the totem pole when compared with the ones I learned while hanging around the blacksmith shop.

The blacksmith often had plenty of reasons to swear. I can recall witnessing a couple of events that provoked his wrath. One occasion occurred a day or two before the Fourth of July. In those days the Fourth was celebrated in a way that was riotous and somewhat dangerous. There was no regulation against the sale of firecrackers and fireworks. The kids usually had a good supply that ranged from bunches of small firecrackers about the size of a stubby pencil to the so-called blockbusters that could be as large as a spray can. When a bucket was set over one of those large ones the explosion was powerful enough to send the bucket eight or ten feet into the air. We had fun, but many fingers were damaged, some quite severely. A few fires were started, horses were spooked into running away, and many people became

disgruntled when small crackers were exploded between their legs. There were usually a number of fights before the day was over. The Fourth was an exciting holiday, well worthy of the event which it celebrated.

On this particular occasion I was at the shop waiting my turn to get one of our horses shod, when a person named Tracy, who lived across the road, visited the place. He was sort of a town character, prone to being a tosspot, and he had started celebrating the Fourth a day or so early. He had a good start, being well primed and in an exuberant mood — one that prevented him from feeling any pain. He had a bag of cherry bombs and accidentally dropped one on the floor. A cherry bomb was a mild device, but the resulting explosion was enough to spook the horses, and the blacksmith was set on his rear end by the horse he was shoeing. Tracy was amused, and he began throwing cherry bombs all over the shop. The place became a bedlam with cherry bombs exploding, horses snorting and jumping around, and the blacksmith swearing a blue streak. He vented his anger against Tracy by grabbing some tongs that were holding a red hot horse shoe in the forge and chasing Tracy out of the shop and across the road where Tracy barricaded himself in his house. The uproar stirred up that section of the village, and it took some time and some choice epithets to quiet things down.

The other memorable occasion involved some oxen that belonged to an old codger known as Uncle Henry, who farmed his small place with them. Oxen need to be shod, but they are much different than horses. They are cloven hoofed, requiring more work and much different shoes than horses. Horses are able to stand on three legs while the fourth one is supported on the blacksmith's knee while it is being fitted with a shoe, but an ox cannot do so. His front and rear quarters

have to be raised and supported by a sling while the shoes are being fitted and applied. An ox in this situation is often restless, and a blacksmith shoeing him, if he is not careful, can find himself in an unpleasant position and exposed to events which can be somewhat calamitous — especially when the beast has been out on green grass. Early green grass has a powerful laxative effect on animals, and anyone shoeing the rear legs of an ox can sometimes have his head right under the gun, so to speak.

On one spring day I was at the shop while Uncle Henry's oxen were being shod, and the inevitable happened. The blacksmith suddenly found himself under a cascade of well-digested green grass. I can see him now, wiping his head and his glasses while his curses rolled across the floor and bounced off of the four walls of the shop. Most of the curses were directed at Uncle Henry who took umbrage at them, saying that he was not in any way responsible for what happened to the insides of a critter.

When the first automobiles began to show up they were more or less experimental, being a duplicate of a buggy with a new source of motive power. They were not built to be propelled over rough and narrow roads instead of being pulled by a plodding horse, or to take to the ditch when it became necessary to make room for others. Their running gear suffered breakage, needing repairs frequently, and the blacksmith shop was at first the only place that could repair them. Broken wheels and axles and other parts were right down the blacksmith's alley, but his knowledge of gasoline motive power was lacking. As the number of automobiles increased and the gasoline age replaced the horse and buggy, the smithy gave way to the garage with its gas pumps and mechanics. The old blacksmith shop, once a vital establishment in every farm community, has vanished and joined the privy and country store as a nostalgic memory of a way of life to the few remaining people who experienced living it at that time.

Telephone

The modern day computer hackers who break into files and obtain private computer information are nothing new; they had their forerunners years ago when telephones and party lines first began to come into use. The modern electronic snoopers are much more sophisticated and dangerous than the nosey old magpies whose worst crime was to listen in on everyone's conversation. According to reports there are people today who have managed to steal credit card numbers and money by way of the Internet, and some day some smart cookie may find a way to screw up the electronic highways and bring the world to a standstill or to disaster. When Alexander Graham Bell invented the telephone, he said that it was an invention which would never be completed. Its marriage to the computer has opened up a Pandora's box, the entire contents of which are as yet unforeseen, and some of its results may not be beneficial. Our dependence on too much technology could someday backfire.

I cannot remember the year when we got our first telephone. It was probably sometime around 1910. The adjoining village of Pike, with which our small village was more or less intertwined, was a world manufacturer of scythestones and had the most modern advances as they became available. Their early telephone system had been extended to include a few places in our small hamlet, and I can remember when people in our district had to go down to the village to make their phone calls.

We did not consider a telephone to be a necessity in those days, and our calls were few in number and were usually made only in case of emergencies. In time the telephone became something more than excess baggage to us, and its line began to be extended up the hills into our area. As I recall, it was sort of a piecemeal extension which was made as different people subscribed for the service. I do not believe that there were more than a dozen places in our district that eventually hooked up to it.

The telephone at that time was an instrument whose innards were enclosed in a cabinet of beautifully grained wood that hung on the wall, and one had to use it while standing. Like most other things in those days it was activated by turning a crank, which caused its bell and all of the other telephone bells on the line to ring.

Most of the early telephone lines were party lines, and our entire district was on the same line. All that had to be done to call anyone who was on the line was to

Station Master's office (1909)
Pike, New Hampshire
Haverhill Hist. Society

ring their number. If a person's number was 13 it meant that one had to make one long ring and then three short ones to alert them that someone wished to talk with them. Sometimes those numbers created great confusion to the old-timers who were not familiar with such a code. Our number was 21, and when an old codger, whose farm was on the mountain in the Limekiln area, first got his phone he called us by ringing the phone twenty-one times.

If someone on a different line wished to talk with you, the call had to go through the central's office where the central operator connected the two lines and did the ringing. The results were the same whoever rang the phone. When one's number rang to alert him that he had a call, it also alerted everyone else on the line to the fact, and there were a number of old busybodies who spent all of their spare time with their telephone receiver glued to their ear listening to other people's conversation. It was called "Rubbering," and if one had anything of a confidential nature to discuss, he didn't want to do it over the telephone. It was no place to converse with a girl friend either. Those old hawks made it a point to learn all that they could of everyone's business and make it a matter of gossip. If my father thought that some old newsmonger was listening on the line, he got a kick out of injecting some outlandish rumor into his conversation and then waiting to see how long it would take for it to be spread around town.

The line was in use a large share of the time by the women of the neighborhood who spent much of their spare moments gossiping with each other. Sometimes there would be three of them conversing together on the line. They were years ahead of the modern telephone conferences, and they were usually long-winded. If one needed to make a call he had to find some way to kick them off the line. Sometimes turning the crank so that the bell rang in their ears would give them enough of a hint. If that didn't work more drastic measures had to be used. At times my grandfather would get so exasperated that he would swear at them. The last resort was to take the receiver off its hook and place it over the mouthpiece of the transmitter. The resulting racket and noise of their own gobbling would literally blast them off the line. The performance usually resulted in a complaint to the central who would call and give you hell for making the interference.

The telephone exchange was located in a small room which was over the store in the adjoining village of Pike. It had a switch board against one wall that sported a number of cables; one for each line that it served. The exchange was manned twenty-four hours a day by central operators who were almost always women, and they usually knew of everything that was going on throughout the countryside. If you were unable to get hold of the doctor the central could tell you where he was, and she would contact him for you. Sometimes she performed heroic deeds in emergencies. If someone's house was on fire, the central would arouse the neighborhood to help fight it.

The exchange room was across the hall from the barber shop, and for a long time there never seemed to be anything very private about it. The door was usually open, and it was interesting to stand at it and watch the central operator manipulating the cables in and out of the holes on the switchboard. She had to be quite dexterous when the lines were busy.

The openness of their operation had an abrupt end when an attractive and friendly young lady was hired to take over the night shift. She had other talents besides running the switch board, and there was a lot of scrambling and competition among the boys vying to be the one who kept her company during the evening hours. After a while people began to complain about the time it took to get her attention. When an investigation by the company uncovered the reason, the operator was replaced and the central's office was put off limits.

Those first rural telephone systems with the overcrowded party lines and the battle to keep one's conversations from becoming public property were much different from the instantaneous electronic procedures that are commonplace today. The results obtained by present technology are amazing, but the operator's voice is probably canned. There is no night operator to spend the evening with, and everything is much more impersonal than it was in the old days. It is not at all as much fun.

Fred Gleason's Store (c. 1900)   E. Whitcher Collection
Warren, New Hampshire

Country Store

Although they served different functions, the old country store and the privy have received about equal attention as representative features of country life as it was lived in the early years. Socially they were the antithesis of each other. The privy was a place of solitude, where one could sit and reflect upon the burdens of the day, whereas the country store offered companionship and a chance to discuss the state of the world with one's fellow man.

The country store was the only spot in our village where daily social contact could be counted on. Our village was a very small place. All it could boast about that resembled industries were a sawmill and a creamery. The main reason for the store's existence was to service the farms of the surrounding countryside.

The only travel that was usually made by the farmers during the day was the morning trip they had to make to deliver their milk to the creamery; some of them had to travel as far as three or four miles. Before returning home they invariably stopped at the store to shop and to pick up any mail (the Post Office was in the store) and to hobnob with the other farmers, exchanging gossip and complaints. In the early morning hours the store was mainly a man's world. There was but little hustle and bustle in the village after the departure of the farmers.

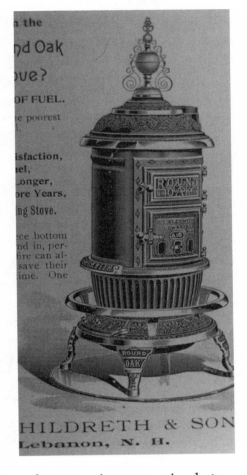

the
nd Oak
ue?

OF FUEL.
e poorest

isfaction,
uel,
Longer,
ore Years,
ng Stove.

ce bottom
nd in, per-
fire can al-
save their
ime. One

HILDRETH & SON
Lebanon, N. H.

Unlike today's stores, whose entire space is cluttered with rows of shelves carrying packaged goods, everything was behind wide counters that were along the rear and two sides of the store. All trades were made over the counter and there was room in front of them to contain the stove and quite a number of people. There was room to rattle around. The hitching racks outside the place were lined with horses, buggies or wagons, and the mornings were the busiest part of the day for the storekeeper.

Activity during the balance of the day was provided mostly by the women who resided in the village and did their shopping and gossiping while awaiting the arrival of the mail. The mail was all carried by the trains in those days. Our small hamlet was only entitled to about four local train stops a day, but the express trains picked up and threw off mail bags as they sped through the village. It was about a quarter of a mile from the railroad station to the post office in the store, and a local resident enjoyed the job of carrying the in-going and out-going mail back and forth between the two places.

The store was usually open during the evening, and it was the only place in the village where the male residents could gather and fraternize. After their evening meal they would usually stroll over to the store to discuss the events of the day and to swap stories. They would sit on the steps in the summer and huddle around the stove in the winter.

Often some of the young blades or hired men who lived on the surrounding farms would drive up to show off their trotters while giving them an evening workout. Contrary to the usual accounts about such gatherings, I never witnessed any checker games. The men usually stood or sat around the place and smoked, while those who chewed tobacco would spit in the sandbox that was set near the stove.

As a social center the store provided entertainment, education, and more. Many fishing and hunting stories were told that were probably greatly exaggerated. The gossip could teach a lot to a kid who kept his ears open. I never worked in a store, but I think I can claim a passing knowledge of the one in our village. For a while I had a yen for one of the girls who occasionally helped out in the place and I used to spend considerable time hanging around the premises.

Many of the accounts of the country stores that I have read stressed the great variety of goods that were stocked. That may have been true of stores in the larger villages, but those that served a countryside of small farms carried only the things that the farmers needed and were unable to produce. There were many more cows than people in our area, and grain accounted for the lion's share of the store's sales. The other necessities that were stocked were flour, sugar, molasses, kerosene, and staples such as tea, coffee, and spices. Farm tools and boots, jackets, and other clothing appeared on the shelves, but their supply was limited. The country store of the early twentieth century had strong competition in such things, and they were careful not to overstock them.

That was the time when the mail order houses of Sears Roebuck and Montgomery Ward were flourishing, and practically everyone received catalogues three or four inches thick, making it hard for the country stores to compete. The catalogues had such a variety of goods and prices, that poring over their contents and making up a wish-list or an order would often provide an evening's entertainment, particularly in the winter.

Mail order companies were particularly frustrating to those storekeepers who were also postmasters. It must have been most exasperating to a postmaster to make out a money order to Sears for someone who also owed him money for unpaid grocery bills. Our storekeeper had some choice names for such people, and was not loathe to express them. He made a practice of taking local produce, such as eggs, butter, potatoes, etc., in trade. When those who patronized the mail order houses approached him on making such trades he would tell them to trade them with Sears Roebuck.

The old time country store was an institution that offered much more than goods for sale. It was the focal point and clearinghouse of practically all of the activity that occurred in the surrounding countryside. The places today that make a point of advertising themselves as such are aimed mostly at the tourist trade. Any real replica of the old country store should be classified as a museum.

UNITED STATES
AND
Canada Express.

Principal Office, 39 and 40 Court Square, BOSTON.

FORWARD TO

NEW HAMPSHIRE — Ashland, Antrim, Beth'ehem, Bradford, Bris-
tol, Canaan, Charlestown, Claremont, Concord, Enfield, Epping,
Fabyan House, Franklin, Groveton, Hanover, Haverhill, Hillsboro'
Bridge, Jaffrey, Keene, Laconia, Lancaster, Lebanon, Littleton,
Manchester, Meredith, Nashua, Newport, No. Weare, Peterboro',
Pittsfield, Plymouth, Portsmouth, Rochester, Tilton, Troy, Warren,
Warner, Weirs, Whitefield.

MASSACHUSETTS — Fitchburg, Greenfield, Lawrence, Lowell,
North Adams, Worcester.

RHODE ISLAND — Providence,

NEW YORK — Albany, Malone, Ogdensburg, Rouse's Point, Troy.

VERMONT — Bellows Falls, Burlington, Hyde Park, Montpelier,
Newport, Rutland, St. Albans, St. Johnsbury, Swanton, White
River Junction, Windsor.

CANADA — Montreal, Sherbrook, St. Johns, Waterloo, P. Q.;
Prescott, P. O., and intermediate places.

CONNECTING WITH OTHER EXPRESSES
To all Accessible Parts of the World.

Railroad

"You can rub and scrub and work like hell,
but you can't get rid of that railroad smell!"

That was either part of a song or a piece of a verse that I can recall. Almost anyone, or anything, or any place, that had an everyday working relationship with the railroad in the days of steam acquired a most distinctive and long lasting odor that came from a mixture of coal and coal dust, smoke, soot, and cinders. The railroad yards, the passenger coaches, the stations, and even the towns that served as busy railroad junctions acquired an aroma that attested to the fact that they were a part of the great transportation network of the country. In the days of steam, when locomotives burned coal, the passengers who patronized the railroads were subjected to the smoke fumes emitted by their smoke-stacks and also to the rocking and swaying of the passenger coaches and their sometimes bone-jarring stops. That is an aspect of the railroad era that nostalgic railroad buffs do not seem to cover.

Railroad enthusiasts are enamored with the huge and powerful locomotives and the luxurious palace cars that they pulled over the rails, including much of the working equipment that was used to operate the trains. The red-chimneyed lanterns that the conductors swung to signal the engineers at night bring a fancy price on today's market, but details of the experiences of the ordinary passengers that rode the rails seem to be lacking.

I have never traveled on any of the present day Amtrak trains, but riding on them cannot be much different from riding the trains almost a century ago.

MANCHESTER LOCOMOTIVE WORKS.

MANUFACTURERS OF

LOCOMOTIVES,

THE "AMOSKEAG" STEAM FIRE ENGINE,

Stationary Steam Engines, and Tools,

MANCHESTER, N. H.

J. A. BURNHAM, Pres't.   W. G. MEANS, Treas.   ARETAS BLOOD, Agent.

It is still steel wheels on steel rails, and the coaches must sway and rumble. The difference is in the motive power. Instead of the large coal-burning locomotives that left plumes of smoke trailing behind them while their huge driving wheels pounded the rails, the cars are pulled by engines that burn diesel oil and that run more smoothly and quietly. Even their whistles are different. Most diesel horns sound like a cow bellowing for her calf. The whistle of a steam locomotive was shrill and piercing; sort of a long, loon-like wail.

The first train ride that is impressed upon my memory occurred when I was about nine or ten years old; I was in knee breeches. I took the train to Boston to visit my aunt and uncle; a four hour trip of about one hundred and fifty miles. It was an event of some consequence as my parents decided that I was old enough to make the trip alone. Most train trips were more or less the same, and an account of the train and my trip can offer some idea of what railroad travel was like.

Our rural village of East Haverhill was on the main line of the Boston & Maine railroad that ran from

Boston to Montreal, and was too small a place to warrant an express stop. I was loaded with my lunch and suitcase onto a local which I think stopped at every station along the way until we reached Lowell. The conductor and brakeman were enjoined to see that I stayed on the train until it reached Boston.

At that time our station was the fourth or fifth stop the train made after leaving Woodsville, where it was first made up. Its beginnings were small. A baggage car and a mail car were the first two cars behind the tender, and they were followed by two or three passenger cars, one of which was reserved for those who smoked. It was known as the smoker, and it reeked to high heaven of tobacco fumes. Cigarette smoking was not very common in those days; one who smoked cigarettes was considered to be a sissy. The people who smoked were mostly older people, and they were addicted to foul-smelling pipes and strong cigars. There were several brass spittoons in the car to enable those who chewed to unload their burden. The tobacco that was consumed was strong and rank and powerful. The car windows were never opened, and the stench of tobacco was strong enough to make some people ill. Present day cigarette smoke, to which so many people object, is extremely mild and almost pleasant compared to the fumes of the harsh tobacco used in those days.

As the train progressed along its way to Boston, more passenger and baggage cars were added and by the time the train left Manchester it was quite a long one, with the coaches pretty well filled with passengers. The addition of more cars seemed to make the ride rougher and noisier. A train ride was never smooth. The railroads prided themselves upon sticking to a time table, and the engineer was responsible for arriving at the various stations on schedule. Often he had to push the engine to make up for lost time. An express train had fewer stops and enough distance between them to enable the engineer to attain and hold a high rate of speed, but locals were required to stop at a station every few miles. By the time the engineer had the train tooling along at a good rate of speed, he had to make a local stop, which often was bone-jarring. As the brakes were applied, each car came to an abrupt stop, often by banging against the coupling of the car in front of it — sort of an accordion stop, and one had to brace himself to prepare for it. People tried to avoid riding in the rear cars for they did the most swaying. Although the conductor was in charge of the train, it was the engineer who had it under his thumb. An engineer with a hangover or in a disgruntled mood could make starting or stopping a ragged procedure.

My aunt was waiting to meet me when the train arrived at North Station. The first thing that she did was to grab me by the ear and lead me to the men's room, where she told me to go in and wash my face. I had committed the sin of opening the car window and sticking my head out of it to observe the sinuous and swaying movements of the train as it rode the rails along the curves. Railroad engines burned coal at that time, and the cars behind them were enveloped in plumes of black smoke and cinders. My face was as black as a boot. I learned then that car windows were not meant to be opened; their only use was for viewing the scenery.

People of means who traveled long distances across the country rode in Pullmans that were heavy cars which rode the rails better, and they were meant to be luxurious. They had one seat on each side of the aisle that was actually a swiveled lounge chair. The Pullman trains had the best engineers, and their crews were especially solicitous of the high fare paying customers. Riding in a Pullman was quite a lot smoother than in a day coach, but they, too, were subject to rough stops and uneven rides.

The people who rode the day coaches for shorter distances did not enjoy the luxuries and attention found in the Pullman cars. The coaches had seats for two on each side of the aisle that were comfortable for an hour or so, but they became pretty tiresome on a three or four hour trip. The cars were lighter in weight than the Pullmans, and they swayed and rocked as they rode the curves. The swaying motion and the click, click, click of the wheels tended to make one drowsy and induced cat naps which were rudely interrupted when the train made a stop.

The conductor and brakemen became used to the swaying motion, and they attained sea legs. They were able to walk down the aisle of a moving car without lurching, but an occasional rider had to steady himself by grabbing the tops of the seats that were on each side of the aisle. A trip down the aisle to the toilet, while the train was moving was a challenge of inching along seat by seat. Each car had a toilet which was a small cubby hole at the end of the car. It had a wash basin and a hopper that emptied between the rails when it was flushed. The trap was wide open, and one could see the railroad bed rushing along underneath it. The brakemen were supposed to lock the door to prevent use of the toilet while the train was stopped at a station, but they were often lax in doing so, and sometimes the train left unpleasant mementos behind for the station agent to clean up.

The station agent was a person of some stature in a small community such as ours. Our agent had more things to take care of than most of the other rural stations on the line. There were only about four trains scheduled to stop at our station daily, but it had the distinction of being a watering stop. It had a high, round water tank which must have held hundreds of gallons of water which were pumped into it from a dammed-up pond on the Oliverian stream. The long

Glencliff Station (c. 1900)
Warren Summit, New Hampshire

E. Whitcher Collection

and heavy freight trains stopped there to take on water for their engines before negotiating the long upgrade to the summit at Glencliff. There was also a siding with several cattle pens which were used by a livestock dealer to hold canners and other useless livestock until they were shipped in car load lots to the city. In addition to performing the duties which those activities required, the agent had to keep his ear attuned to the clacking of the telegraph which was continually carrying messages and train orders over its wires. In the years before the telephone arrived, the telegraph was the only link which the rural areas had to communicate with the rest of the country. Until the baseball games were broadcast over the radio, people crowded the railroad stations to get the play by play description of the World Series as it came over the wires.

Like most memories of the past, the uncomfortable aspects of railroad travel are only evident when viewed in retrospect. At that time travel by rail offered the only practical way to go any distance. It was the only game in town, and the things that seem unpleasant to us now were accepted as commonplace in those days. They were overshadowed by the thrill and excitement that was generated by traveling at what was then considered to be a high rate of speed.

The huge and powerful locomotives and the men who drove them occupied somewhat the same niche as that of the present-day astronauts and the rockets that propel them into space. It was most every kid's ambition to be an engineer. Known in railroad circles as a "hogger," he made his presence known every time he went through an area. It was a rule of law for a train to whistle before every crossing, and each engineer had his signature. There was one run through our valley that was known as the Montreal Express. It rumbled over the two crossings in our area just before midnight. The sound of the huge driving wheels pounding the rails became increasingly louder as the northbound train roared down the grade from the Summit, and it and the whistles at the crossings awoke most of the countryside. One could tell by his whistle who was at the throttle. Lying in bed and listening to the echo of the long, loon-like wail of the whistle bouncing off the hills of the valley is my most lasting recollection of the days of the steam railroad era.

Hard Sledding

Aside from wars, probably the most distressing experience the country suffered in this century was the Depression of the 1930's. For many people it was the darkest period of their lives. Although their ranks are thinning, there are still many who remember what it was like. No part of the country was immune from it. The people who lived in the cities and the places that depended upon manufacturing and heavy industry for their existence suffered the hardships that resulted from the loss of jobs and the lack of money. Even harder times were endured by the people who were battered by the disaster of the dust bowl and the failure of the farms of the grain belt.

Books have been written that deal with the causes, economics and politics of the disaster. Franklin Roosevelt has been both damned and praised for the administrative changes he made in an effort to combat it. The woes and tribulations of many of the individuals who were affected by the Depression have been recorded in many accounts and pictures, but with the exception of the dust bowl and the farm foreclosures, there are few accounts of the way those in rural areas of the country coped with the hard times. The people who lived in the rural, one-horse backwaters such as our area of New England hillside farms were made aware of the Depression in various ways. However, they had had plenty of practice in wresting a living from the stony hillsides and were well conditioned to lean pickings.

Most of the farms in our area produced milk for the dairy industry, and they had suffered from low prices for some years prior to 1930. There were many cities in New England that were dependent upon the textile industry, and they experienced their own depression when the large mills began to close and move south during the last years of the 1920's. The farmers who depended upon their markets suffered accordingly. Many small dairy farmers in our area had sold their herds, and had been eking out a living by subsisting on the land while they picked up what work they could find. Hard sledding had been more or less normal to them for some time, and they managed to take the big Depression in their stride. The rural areas often proved to be a boon to others who were experiencing stress. At that time there were quite a number of people living in the cities who had some sort of tie to the land through relatives who had a farm, which in many cases became a haven of refuge to them.

There were no soup kitchens or bread lines in our countryside. Practically everyone, even in the small towns and villages, had land enough for a garden, and it doesn't take much room for a few chickens. There were rabbits, which became known as "Hoover's beef," and birds in the woods, and a knowledgeable person could manage to find larger game which was often shared with others. One had to be lazy or a pretty poor shot to go hungry. People pooled both their resources and their troubles.

Hoover's Beef

However, the economic stagnation of the Depression was far-reaching enough to have an impact on our region. It was not exactly a paradise. By then the change in living customs had begun to penetrate our area. Subsistence farms were still a dominant way of life, but there were people who had left them and depended upon a steady job instead of the land for their living. A lot of people worked for the railroad. Others worked in the woods and in sawmills and in other small factories and businesses that had become established over the years. All such places suffered from the poor economic conditions. None of them were thriving. Many were forced to curtail or close, and some went broke.

Jobs became infrequent and intermittent. They were low-paying, even for those days, and cash was hard to come by. People were scared, and those who had managed to accumulate any money kept it under their mattress. It didn't circulate very freely. Barter, in both work and goods, was common. The country store keepers, who were numerous at that time, were well acquainted with the people of the area, and they extended credit to the needy. They often did so to their own detriment, and they have not been credited with the merit that they deserve for the part they played in helping those who were in need. It is hard to imagine today's large supermarkets playing such a role.

As I recall, there were not many farm foreclosures in our region, as a lot of people owned their farms outright. To many, a mortgage was something to be avoided in those days. However, if they were producing milk, their livestock was the first to go, and some farms and woodlots and a lot of timberland were sold for taxes. Many of the farms somehow managed to hang on until Roosevelt's Farm Credit Bank eased their situation. The first two or three years were the hardest. The large, bellwether companies laid off people and workers by the thousands. Banks were closing all over the country, and many people lost everything in the way of money that they had. Like a snowball rolling down hill, the Depression grew upon itself until it crushed every section of the country, both urban and rural.

Many of the reports of that time create a picture of brokers and bankers jumping out of high story windows; of people begging in the streets; of families and children on the edge of starvation; and of farmers with shotguns fighting to save their neighbor's farm from foreclosure and the auction block. Those events were true, and happened often enough to lend an air of discouragement and dejection to the era, but there was another side to the picture.

A large number of people were resilient and attempted to combat their troubles. Many who became unemployed in the cities started selling apples and other things on street corners, and using whatever talents they had to eke out an existence. We did not have any street corners in the country, but there were people who emulated the old-time Yankee peddlers by traveling the countryside trying to sell whatever they could manage to produce. A person in one of our adjacent towns dug and processed horseradish, which he peddled from door to door. Until he could do better, he traveled on foot with a pack on his back. Another person, who had an old truck, raised corn which he processed into hulled corn, a product of bygone days. It was cheap and filling, and people found that they liked it. He did quite well at selling it. Some small farmers butchered animals which they raised and started regular routes, selling the meat door to door. I remember one person who tuned pianos. He trudged the roads looking for jobs, and would tune a piano for a meal or a night's lodging and breakfast, and any money that people felt they could afford to give him. For some strange reason people all over the country became addicted to a jigsaw puzzle craze. They bought and swapped and traded

them in great numbers. One person in our village became adept at making them and sold all that he could
turn out.

There were people who became outlaws of a sort
in trying to make ends meet. Prohibition was in effect
until the end of 1933. There were a few who started
running small stills and sold their product to the bootleggers, or else became bootleggers themselves. We had
a neighbor up the road from us who had worked down-
country in his younger days for a large brewery, and he
knew how to make decent beer. He sold it by the bottle
or by the bucket. When the weather was cold enough
to freeze deer carcasses, a few venturesome souls
smuggled venison to the cities.

The attempts to earn a little money were many
and varied, and almost everything was tried. No one
became affluent in his activities, but the struggle to
make ends meet seemed as beneficial to a person's well-
being as the pittance which he earned. Prices were
unbelievably low. The man of the song who asked for a
dime did not appear to be asking for much by today's
standards, but ten cents
was worth struggling for
at that time. It would
buy two loaves of bread.
Time-Life Magazine has
published a picture of a
menu which was chalked
on the window of a
restaurant of those days.
A person had several
choices of dinner for a
dime. One could buy a
dinner of franks and
kraut, a vienna roast, or
meat balls and beans.

Two eggs, potatoes and coffee could be purchased for ten cents, or a bowl of soup and bread for a nickel. Anyone affluent enough to spend twenty cents could buy a dinner of roast sirloin, corned beef and cabbage, lamb chops, or ham and eggs. Even at those prices there were many who went hungry. A barber shop in the same picture offers a shave and a haircut for thirty cents. Today most shops consider a shave beneath their dignity.

The basic functions of the country had to be met, although they were greatly curtailed. Anyone who had a paying job was favored by the Depression. Salaries and wages were low, but so were prices, and those who were at the right place at the right time enjoyed quite a degree of prosperity. I was one of the fortunate ones. A couple of years or so before the Crash of 1929 I began work for the New Hampshire Forestry Department and the Department of Agriculture. They were cooperating in combating the white pine blister rust disease, which was spreading rapidly. My work with them involved mapping the forest cover of different areas of the state ahead of their crews. At first the work was intermittent, but I practiced land surveying on the side. As the Depression progressed there were a few long periods between jobs, but I was living on the farm with my parents. My father was one of those who had stopped dairying some years before, but the farm still produced enough so that we were comfortable. When President Roosevelt started his projects to put people to work, I became involved in some of them. I was employed in Warren, N.H., in one of the first CCC camps, laying out roads in the National Forest. Later I worked on a survey of the rural areas of the state.

I look back upon that period as one of the most pleasant times of my life. It was then that I became involved in large-scale logging operations, an occupation which I followed for about twenty-five years.

The paper companies continued buying pulpwood, but the price which they paid us for cutting and delivering it was ridiculously low. Manpower was plentiful. We had "no men wanted" signs at the entrances of all of our tote roads. As I recall, our jobbers charged fifty cents a day for board. If a man produced enough wood to pay for his board and wangan and have a little money left over, he was doing well.

When Roosevelt took office in 1933 and began to involve the government in providing relief and instituting his New Deal and its make-work policies, people began to regain some degree of confidence. Those who had money began taking it from under their mattresses and putting it to work. Conditions began to improve and gradually began to right themselves. However, Depression conditions persisted until the end of the 1930's. The hurricane of 1938 gave our area a strong shot in the arm by providing jobs in salvaging the great amount of timber that it had blown down, but it took the beginning of World War II in Europe to really start things rolling throughout the country.

I am not an economist or a sociologist or any other sort of an "ist," but in looking back it appears to me that Roosevelt put his finger on one of the root problems of the Depression — at least one that prolonged it — when he said that "the only thing we have to fear is fear itself." People were scared. Jobs were going down the drain by the thousands, and one never knew when he would be idled. There was no unemployment insurance or public welfare. Many banks were going under; even some of the solvent ones were forced to close when people made runs upon them and withdrew their money. They bought gold with it or put it under their mattress.

Many people discovered that the best things in life are free, and that there were many things that they could do without and still find life enjoyable. They confined their buying to bare essentials. The frivolous and unnecessary things that people are conned into buying are really amazingly numerous, and the resulting effect upon the economy when their purchase is discontinued can be disturbing.

Roosevelt's policies resulted in restoring some confidence, and money began coming out from the hidden places and was again put to use. He had many opponents who criticized him for creating a deficit. Government figures are unreliable, but according to the treasury figures which I have seen, the total deficit during his first eight years was less than twenty billion dollars. It was a big figure then, but today's Solons must consider him a piker.

The policies which he created were needed at that time. However, over the years many of Roosevelt's innovations have been expanded by the people and their politicians to an extent that far exceeds the purpose for which they were intended. His policies have been applied to so many people in so many ways that they have become a grab bag, and in addition they have spawned huge and useless bureaucracies, all of which have become too costly and too burdensome to those who are productive. We are reaching the point where something is going to have to give somewhere. It is taking too much money to make the mare go.

Mountain Years

Introduction to Mountain Years

I will testify that everything Bill Morse writes about Moosilauke is true. Bill spent three boyhood summers at the summit, 1915–1917, helping his parents run the rustic hotel there — the old Moosilauke Tip Top House — when he was just the right age to explore the place to the full. Any admirer of the Moosilauke summit will have to envy that unique experience, and be grateful to Bill for bringing it alive for us.

My own focus on the mountain is a pale reflection of Bill's, but it does include the Summit House (as we came to call it) and its bob-tailed cats. When I came along a couple decades after Bill, the mountain and the Summit House were hardly whittled down one millionth of a meter from his days. Between Bill's 80 years on and off the mountain and my 60, we total 140 we can talk about together.

Our family usually climbed the mountain on the Benton trail. If you know that trail, you may know the little mossy spring off to the right where in a good year you could get a nice drink of water. It was at that spring, some years before Bill's time, that my father, Stearns Morse, pulled out his watch, and off fell the crystal. The little blue second hand dropped into the green moss, surely lost. But no, his sister, my Aunt Susie, had eyes that could reliably find four-leafed clovers in the lawn. Those eyes found the second hand, which was soon restored to its spindle by the Woodsville watchmaker.

Bill and his family moved their goods up to the summit by the Carriage Road, of course, and he describes in awful detail what a rough trip that was. Just over a decade later, the first downhill ski race in America was run on that Carriage Road, and many will have seen the funny films of that day and era. By the 1950's the road was so ingrown and washed out that even with more modern equipment, we could hardly make all the corners, and had to rely on tree-hugging to slow down. Now, I am told, the road has been rebuilt, cut clear of encroaching trees, bulldozed, and smoothed. Oh, what a sight that must be, and when will we get to see it, Bill?

Jobildunk Ravine had a special place in Bill Morse's life, and in mine. As he tells here, he made his own trail there and got down over the headwall somewhat farther and faster than he intended. I first came the other direction. In the late forties working up through the Ravine past the abandoned logging Camp 3, on a trail crew from the Ravine Camp, we got hot enough to climb up onto the headwall and shower in the icy little waterfall. One of our jobs was to take apart the remains of Camp 3, the big horse barns and the cookhouse, and to pull the nails out of the lumber. Camp 3 was on the floor of Jobildunk Ravine, a big, wide-open, flat place with plenty of space for buildings and log yards and miles of open sky. You try to go there today and you can't even see the sky for the spruce jungle, much less believe there was a big logging camp there. Most of the skylight came in with the 1938 Hurricane, the one that got Bill started working in the woods.

A decade later, out of the site of Camp 3, we built the Ridge trail, slabbing up onto the Blue Ridge and connecting with the Beaver Brook trail that leads either back up to the summit, or down to Kinsman Notch and Beaver Pond. I envied Bill Morse again on reading how he guided people for day-trips down to Lost River over the easier logging roads instead of down the precipitous Beaver Brook trail. One of my daughters and I have long had a secret wish to blaze a trail down to Bungay along some of the same lines. Bungay? Wildwood to you younger people.

Thomas Jefferson said he'd sooner believe Yankee Professors would lie than believe stones fell out of the sky, and some may think this Yankee Professor would lie about somebody with the same name from the same town almost. But just as meteorites do fall from the sky, Bill Morse's truths fall from his pen unadorned by hogwash, and they need no defense from me. He worked for four decades with my family's close friend in Bath Upper Village, Paul Glover, but our lives were separate until a quarter century ago, when Bill was pretty young. Then he taught me how to count chain lengths by shifting pennies from one pocket to the other as we surveyed my father's birthplace so's to put it back into the family. He wrote on the map, "Fence meanders with line", and maybe that will be the title of his next book when he tells us more about his life as a surveyor.

And if you think we're related, well no and then a little bit yes. Bill Morse's great grandfather built the Tip Top House, but the Wood-worths eventually owned it and the summit land, and gave them to Dartmouth College. My Mother's brother Winthrop Field married Pauline Woodworth; we grew up hearing about those remarkable peo-ple and the coincidence that we were sort of married into our favorite mountain. When we climbed the mountain, we signaled home at noon from the summit with a mirror, and Mom flashed back with her bed-room mirror. And I like to say that I saw the Summit House burn — many times, as the red sunset was reflected from its windows to our Farm. People from as far away as Bradford and Newbury know the great, looming massif of Moosilauke as their Mountain, and they will be enchanted to read Bill's reminiscences. With me, they will envy his childhood summers on the summit, which he knew as nobody ever, before or since, could have known. Thanks, Bill, for this treasure.

Stearns A. Morse
Goose Lane Farm
Swiftwater, New Hampshire

(Tony Morse is Professor of Geology at UMass/Amherst, and a writer for numerous publications, including *Smithsonian Magazine*.)

Tip Top House
Mt. Moosilauke

A. E. Morse, Mgr.
P. O. Address   Warren, N. H.

July 1st 1915.   Change in management of Tip Top House on Mount Moosilauke, now open for the season.

Parties desiring transportation from Warren are requested to notify E. R. Whitcher, Warren, New Hampshire.

Rates, $3.00 per day   Supper, Breakfast
and Room, $2.50   Special Parties, $2.00

Correspondence May Be Addressed To
A. E. Morse   Warren, New Hampshire
E. B. Mann   Woodsville, New Hampshire

Moosilauke

ew Hampshire has a mountain that bears the name of Moosilauke: a name of Indian origin. Geologic upheavals and erosions of the ages have made it one of the dominant features of the landscape, and endowed it with a view that many claim to be unsurpassed in New England. From 1860 to 1942 a house was perched on the highest point of the mountain, which is over 4800 feet above sea level. From a crude, one story structure of stone, the house evolved into a two-and-one-half story hostelry that was well patronized in an era of White Mountain history; an era that has long since disappeared. For three summers, when I was in my early teens — 1915, 1916, and 1917 — my parents managed the hostelry which was known as the Tip Top House, and I enjoyed the privilege of living on the

Mooscoog Mtn.

T. Pownal (1776)

mountaintop. Now, after the passage of around eighty years, it seems appropriate to jot down something of the mountain and to recall some of my memories of those years.

By New England standards Moosilauke is an immense mountain: one of the high peaks of the northeast. There are a few peaks that are higher in elevation, but there are none that can offer such an extensive and intimate view of New England, and also part of Canada and New York. Standing on its crest on a crystal clear day can be likened to standing under the dome of an immense, inverted bowl whose rim, at every point of the compass, is far away in spatial distance. The eastern part of its rim extends over and beyond the peaks of Mt. Washington and the Presidential Range of the White Mountains and reaches into Maine. As it circles easterly and southerly, the circumference of its rim touches the Atlantic Ocean, sweeps around Wachusett and Greylock in Massachusetts, and in the west it disappears behind the high peaks of the Adirondacks. The rim completes its circuit by encompassing the most northerly peaks of the Green Mountains of Vermont, Owl's Head in Canada, the upper reaches of the Connecticut River, and it skirts the Umbagog region and embraces a large part of the Mahoosucs before it makes its closure.

The first known written record of the Indian name of the mountain — as far as my knowledge goes — appears on a map bearing the date 1776, entitled "A Map of the MIDDLE BRITISH COLONIES IN NORTH AMERICA .... By T. POWNAL, MP." The map is accompanied by a topographical description, part of which states that in Lat. 44 the land rises into a high tract called *Mooscoog Mountain*, and that is the name that appears on the map. The name is not too dissimilar from its present one of Moosilauke. The discrepancy in the last syllable can probably be explained by the fact

107

that the Indians ended their words on a low-pitched note, not easily deciphered by an untrained ear, and the early cartographer did the best that he could in interpreting it.

It has been claimed that Moosilauke means "Bald Place." However, the word "Moos" meant moose in the Abenaki dialect, and to many people the most logical meaning of the name is "Moose Place." It was moose range. Little's *History of Warren* tells us that the first white settler to stand on the crest of the mountain was a young man named Chase Whitcher, who was pursuing a moose across the peak.

As the early settlements grew, people became interested in ascending the mountain, and two trails were cut for their convenience. One, which history tells us was cut with the aid of a keg of rum, traversed the southwest slope, starting at Ben Little's tavern at Warren Summit, which is now Glencliff. Later, when the Merrill Farm was settled in East Warren, a bridle path from it to the top was swamped up the southeast side. From that time to the present day the town of Warren has been the focal point of those interested in Moosilauke, and the mountain seems to belong to it more than it does to the town of Benton in which the peak and most of its mass is located. The arrival of the railroad in 1851 resulted in a comfortable and fast mode of travel that brought in people from afar who were interested in the mountain country. Inns and hotels were built to accommodate them, and in 1860 a house was built upon the crest of the mountain.

When the town of Coventry, which later became Benton, was first surveyed and divided into lots around 1790, the area encompassing the huge mass of Moosilauke was not lotted. Instead, it became undivided land, the ownership of which was represented by a number of shares that were later rounded up and acquired by an enterprising Yankee trader named Ira Whitcher.

Ira Whitcher

The Boston, Concord and Montreal Railroad purchased about one half of those shares from Whitcher, and thus obtained a sizable stake in the mountain. A case can be made that it was probably the railroad that first broached the idea of accommodations for food and lodgings on its peak. Whatever the reason, enough interest was soon aroused to cause two adventurous souls from Warren, Darius Swain and James Clement, to construct a house on the highest point of the mountain. The house was opened with a big celebration in July of 1860 under the name of The Prospect House. Darius Swain was my great grandfather. Unfortunately, he did not live to share in the fruits of his labor, as he died the year after the house was built. Perhaps the celebration was too much for him.

The first building was a simple structure, about thirty by seventy feet. Its walls, which were about three feet thick, were built entirely of stones which were gathered from the mountaintop. It had the distinction of being the first mountaintop winter residence used by scientific observers in New England, and probably in the United States. During the winter of 1869–70, Professor J. H. Huntington of Dartmouth College and Amos F. Clough, a photographer from Warren, occupied the house, making observations and experiencing the severe winter weather which is common to a mountain of that altitude.

Moosilauke Prospect House (c. 1860's)

Moosilauke Tip Top House (late 1890's)

Ezra B. Mann

The house proved to be so popular in the summers that it had to be enlarged, first in 1881 with the addition of a frame building. A two and a half story wooden structure was added on to the old stone building in 1901, raising the rooflines to the same height. Along the way the Moosilauke Hotel Company and Moosilauke Road Company were incorporated, and the house became known as the Tip Top House.

In 1915 a family friend, Ezra B. Mann, prevailed upon my parents to take over the summer management of the house. He was a druggist in Woodsville, and was a shareholder in the company that owned the property. My father was recovering from a bout with pneumonia that left him unable to carry on the farming and logging which he had been accustomed to doing. The Tip Top House had not been run successfully for some years, and the arrangement for my parents to take over its management appeared to offer benefits to both my father and the Company.

We made our first ascent of the mountain early in May in 1915, and I imagine that my parents had second thoughts about their agreement to manage the place. Our route was by the carriage road that ran from Breezy Point, a resort at the foot of the mountain in Warren, to the top, which is in Benton. It was supposed to be five miles, but few ever hiked it who thought it was less than eight. I remember that ascent very well, for we began to think that we would never reach the top.

Tip Top House (1915)

In the doorway – my mother (Mabel Morse), and next to her Ina House (her housekeeper), myself, Ora Lavoie (helper), and in front, my father (Albert Morse) and Dinah the Cow.

Bill and Albert Morse (c. 1912)

We occasionally got a glimpse of the top and the house, and each time that we did, they seemed to be as far away as they had been an hour before. The road was built in 1870, for the purpose of transporting guests and supplies up the mountain, and in our time it was showing its age. It was traveled by a stage, which was a two-seated contraption called a buckboard that was pulled by a pair of horses. Early accounts, which were probably publicity splurges generated by the railroad, praised the stage as a pleasant way of getting to the top of the mountain. Whoever wrote them must have done so with his tongue in his cheek.

A buckboard, a vehicle of ancient usage, was a platform of springy boards with a set of wheels attached to each end. Samuel Drake, who rode up the mountain around 1882, described it as one of the most ill-favored things he had ever seen, and wrote at that time that the road was no bed of roses. I never rode on the rig, but guests who did often complained of the jolting that they received. A person named Harry Fifield owned and operated the stage. The platform on the buckboard which he used when we were on the mountain was

Moosilauke Carriage Road (1890's)

extra long to handle both supplies and passengers, and
it was exceptionally springy. If it traveled at any sort
of speed when descending the mountain, the ones
riding in it must have resembled dice being shaken in
a chuckaluck cage. The stage accompanied us on our
first trip, carrying our supplies. We walked, and we
rarely traveled the carriage road after that first ascent
as we found the Glencliff trail to be much shorter.

The house was shuttered and closed during the
winter months, and getting it ready for guests required
a lot of work each spring. The roofs usually needed
attention. The interior had a strong, musty smell and

required cleaning and airing out. The carriage road and the telephone line which followed it from Breezy Point suffered from winter storms and needed a lot of work. We hired two or three men each spring to fix them. Once repaired, the telephone line would give us contact with the world below, but a couple of severe storms would render it useless and it would be out for the rest of the season.

All of our supplies came up by stage, and they had to be scheduled to meet our needs. The Woodworths were large shareholders in the hotel. They had a wholesale grocery house in Woodsville that was the source of most of our supplies. Each spring the warehouse was supposed to mark and identify the boxes that contained our essential food stuffs so that they would arrive at the house the same day that we did. The second spring we opened the house someone mismarked the boxes, and all that we received that could be called food was salt codfish and crackers. Harry said that he would open the boxes before his trip the next day so that we would be sure of having food. The next day turned out to be three or four days, as a storm came up that was severe enough to prevent the stage from making the trip. Harry made a couple of efforts, but had to turn back. During that time we subsisted on salt codfish and crackers! I do not recommend it as a steady diet, and I have never been fond of either of them since that time.

I celebrated my eleventh, twelfth, and thirteenth birthdays on August eighteenth of each of the three years that we were on the mountain. On two of them we had snow: no great amount, but the ground was white — water froze. Each year we went up to prepare for the season around the middle of May. The end of the season depended upon the weather, but it was usually near the first of October. In those days it was easy to get excused from school for work on the farm or elsewhere, and I was able to duck two or three weeks at each end of the school year. It didn't seem to be detrimental to my education — or to the school.

I was the only kid on the mountain — alone and footloose. I had a collie dog named Ted, and we roamed Moosilauke whenever and wherever we pleased. My parents were never certain of where we were, and there must have been times when they worried about us. I had spent some time hanging around my father's logging jobs, and I knew something about the woods; at least I thought I did. I had read Nessmuck, an authority on woods lore at that time, and fancied myself well prepared for any emergency. I carried a small axe, a supply of dry matches and a candle, and some milk chocolate for rations. I usually had some rope with me that was used to bundle up any dry firewood that I could handle and drag home. Firewood was one of our biggest problems. The peak of Moosilauke is above timberline and is bare and firewood was a precious commodity. I was always on the lookout for it, and my contributions to the woodpile were helpful.

Mother, Dad, Ora, and Ted (my collie)

My dog and I had numerous adventures while exploring the mountain. We got into some difficult places. I remember a day when we went down the West Slide. From the top we could look down the slide and see the roof of an old abandoned logging camp on Slide Brook. So, we went down to investigate, and we had a devil of a time getting back. The slide was so steep and rough that we were unable to return the way we went down, and we had to find another way home.

In all of our travels on the mountain there was only once when we experienced serious trouble. An old scrap book at the house had a description of trails that had been used in the past. Most of them had been abandoned and unused for years. I re-opened many of them. While opening one that led to Jobildunk Ravine, my dog, who was running ahead of me, suddenly disappeared into thin air! He had gone over the headwall which is practically a sheer drop of over 150 feet. It is another drop of about 300 feet to the floor of the ravine, and I figured that Ted was a goner until I heard him bark. Fortunately, he had landed on a small ledge that protruded in from the side about halfway down. With the aid of my firewood rope I was able to reach him, and found him bruised but unharmed. The only direction we could go to get out of there was up, and we had to fight and claw our way back to the top. I later learned that sometime in the past a lookout with an iron railing had been built there. The old abandoned trail that I had been re-opening once led to it. I found two pieces of the iron railing that had been driven into the ledge, and I suppose they are still there.

There are legends about gold on the mountain. There is one about one of Rogers' Rangers who supposedly traveled over Moosilauke on his way home from the raid on St. Francis and found gold. My father used to tell of an Indian who lived in Warren who would go

117

North Side – Some of the firewood we had to cut is seen here. The attached privy is on the left.

Treeline – Only a few of the old trees were available nearby for firewood, so dry fuel generally had to be gathered further down the mountain.

onto Moosilauke and return with gold. People tried to follow him and learn his secret, but he always gave them the slip. I never looked for gold in my wanderings around the mountain, for I never knew what to look for or how to do so. In recent years people have panned gold out of Baker River in the Moosilauke area, but I believe that its association with granite makes it difficult to refine.

The few chores which were assigned to me were not very demanding. Aside from rounding up firewood while on my travels, I had to wipe dishes and help tend the office when we were busy. One weekly chore which I performed was that of visiting the South Peak and viewing our farm through field glasses. We could not see it from the main peak as the Hogback range blocked it from our view. If she was not busy, my mother often accompanied me. My father had kept just enough of the farm going to keep the hired man occupied. The hired man was an institution in those days, and was usually considered as part of the family. It is an occupation that has disappeared with the passage of time.

The old unused trails which I re-opened led to many scenic spots of the mountain which had not been visited for years and had become unknown. Those guests who made extended stays were interested in viewing them, and they made the house their headquarters for other side trips around the area, and I acted as a guide. I used to take guests down to Lost River, and often took them through it. At the time we went on the mountain the route down to Kinsman Notch was pretty obscure. Logging operations had made that part of the mountain a pretty gray area, and there was nothing that could be called a trail. As I recall, the present Beaver Brook trail was established the second or third year that we were on the mountain, but it was too steep for our liking. Our route was by way of the Benton trail for a

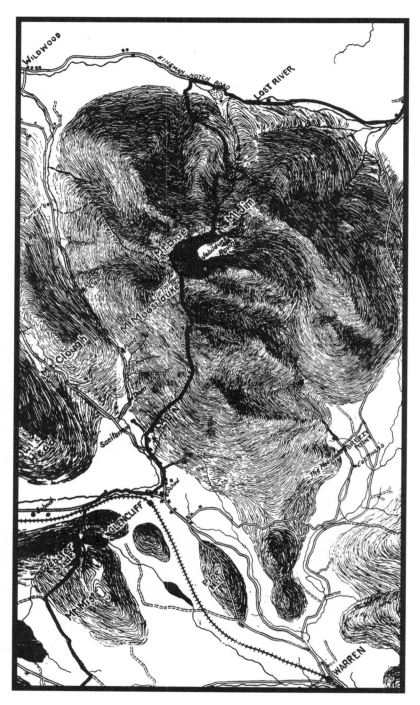

Moosilauke and Environs
Dartmouth Outing Club trail map (1915)

Bert Gilbert

short
distance,
and then we
cut over to Mt.
Blue where we could
follow the rough lumber
roads down to Kinsman Notch.

Guiding guests around the
mountain proved to be rewarding, and
at times I was quite busy at it. There are places on
Moosilauke that would give any spot in the White
Mountains strong competition if they were more accessible. Places such as the Nine Cascades on Little Tunnel,
the Seven Cascades known as the Pleiades on Gorge
Brook, and Jobildunk Ravine and its cascades are scenic,
and at times they are spectacular. During the summer
months when there is not much water going over them
they are rather tame, but in heavy cloudbursts and
during the spring run-offs they are host to a mighty
torrent of water. In the springtime such a torrent of
water pours over the Nine Cascades in Little Tunnel
that it is visible from Route 112 in Wildwood.

There are many stone cairns on the mountain. The small ones were built to mark the location of the trails where they traverse the bare peak above timberline. There are a number of them marking a route up the cone from the south. The Benton and Beaver Brook trails cross the bare peak for quite a distance after they leave timberline, and the cairns are necessary in order to follow the trail when heavy clouds cover the mountain. When we were on the mountain, there were large cairns which were probably built to hold the signal staffs when the mountains were first triangulated by the Coast Survey around 1873. There was one such cairn on the South Peak and there was also one, which I have been told has since disappeared, on the East Peak of Moosilauke. That one had some white quartz stones as a cap, which made it readily identifiable, and there is a story about it — one which did not fully unfold itself to me until about three years ago.

One day my dog, Ted, and I went fishing in Baker River along the stretch below the Jobildunk Cascades. Trout were abundant in those days. There are reports of people catching more than they could carry home. We left the river to return to the house because of a storm that was threatening, and it hit us about halfway up the

mountain. A heavy cloud enveloped us, and visibility was not much more than fifty feet. It is easy to become disoriented under such conditions, and after ascending to a somewhat level spot I was confused and uncertain of where we were. We were pretty well lost. We stumbled around and suddenly came upon the cairn with the white stones upon it. I knew then that we were on the East Peak and within easy distance of home. The entire story was revealed to me about three years ago when I read an account written by Daniel Q. Clement in 1879. He and his brother, James, spent a full year on top of the mountain. James Clement ran the Tip Top House for so many years that he became known as the old man of the mountain. Daniel Q. kept an account during the year that they lived there, part of which is as follows: "There is a pile of rocks laid up by Mr. Sawyer down on the east ridge. He set them up with such skill that the pile looks like a tall shaft to mark the spot where the coast men did their hard work. I go down and put a white cap of quartz rocks on its top. How fine it looks now." Daniel's cap of white rocks also looked mighty fine to a boy and his dog some thirty-five years later when they were lost and uncertain of the way home! It is strange that such a landmark should disappear, and it is hard to understand why anyone would destroy it. It must have taken some effort to tear it down.

The large White Mountain hotels of that era were palatial in size and services. Compared to them, the Tip Top House was like an overgrown farmhouse. However, my parents were the sort to make it homey and comfortable, and it acquired a reputation for hospitality. Its office and entrance were in the wooden portion that faced south. The stone part of the original building contained the kitchen, dining room, washroom and toilets. It also contained the laundry which was entered through the door on the south end. The walls of the stone part were

Privy

Shed

and

Storage

EAST

Dining Room

Kitchen

Storage

Wash
Room

Laundry

Desk

Library

Office
and
Lounge

WEST

—1915 Moosilauke —
—Tip Top House —
— First Floor —

very thick, and the window sills were at least three feet wide. They could serve as a seat or a small table. The kitchen had a long half window whose sill was about four feet from the floor. That window sill became my domain. In stormy weather I spent many hours curled up on it reading books from the library.

There was a fine library at the house. This also served as a lounge and adjoined the office. The wall between the two rooms was shelved from floor to ceiling, and it was full of books which had accumulated over the years. Both it and the office had tables and easy chairs. They faced southerly and westerly, receiving a lot of sun, and they were pleasant and comfortable. We depended on kerosene lamps and lanterns for our lights. There were chandeliers in the office, and large Aladdin lamps in the library that gave a lot of light. The authors that I recall and which I devoured were Alexander Dumas, Francis Parkman, and Thoreau. Ernest Thompson Seton and Nessmuck were there,

Through the three-foot thick stone wall of the kitchen there was a broad window shelf, which became one of my favorite spots for reading. (Bill Morse's model is now at the Warren Hist. Society.)

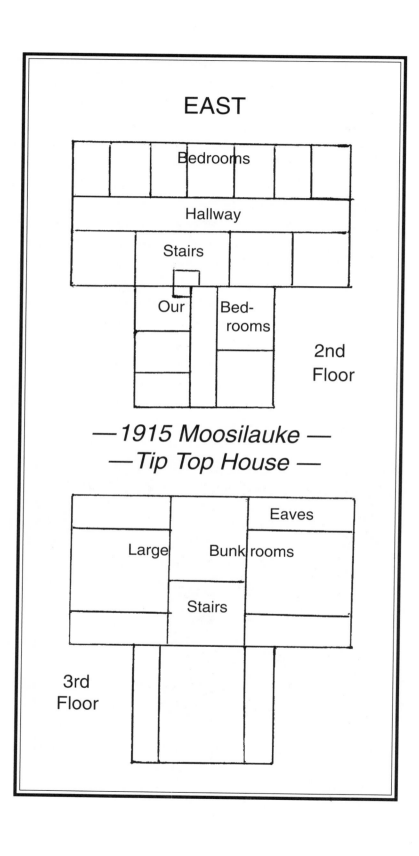

EAST

Bedrooms

Hallway

Stairs

Our

Bed-
rooms

2nd
Floor

— *1915 Moosilauke* —
— *Tip Top House* —

Eaves

Large

Bunk rooms

Stairs

3rd
Floor

along with Jack London and Arsène Lupin. In years past Lucy Larcom had been a steady habituée of the mountain, and I guess all of her writings were there. My mother was one of her avid admirers, and made me read all of her accounts that were at the library and in the old registers. That library was sort of a teenager's paradise.

The bedrooms were small and were meant only for sleeping. They were sparsely furnished with only a bed, stand, washbowl, and a thundermug. The four large, mostly open places on the third floor were intended for groups. The girls' and boys' camps bargained for special rates and were given those rooms. The counselors preferred to have their charges bunk in groups as they could control them better. The members of those camps were quite frolicsome and noisy and often disturbed the regular guests. Sometimes my father had to step in and help the counselors quiet them down. The girls' camps were worse than the boys'!

The summer hotel at the foot of the mountain, Breezy Point, later renamed the Moosilauke Inn, was about halfway between Warren and the Tip Top House. Many people who used the stage would stay there overnight instead of trying to make the full trip to the top in one day. There were occasions when the stage trip up the mountain could be an adventurous ordeal. As the road rose above timberline it traversed a long, narrow ridge which had sharp and steep drop-offs on each side. When the stage encountered clouds and violent wind storms, as they often did, the passengers were thankful when they reached the haven of the house.

There were some guests who stayed with us for a week or longer. Two women were so enamored of the mountain that they stayed for a month or more each summer. My mother said they were connected with Shippens College, and she thought one of them was the Dean.

THE MOOSILAUKE,
Breezy Point, N. H.

The Moosilauke
Breezy Point.
N H.

THIS house accommodates 100 guests and is situated at an elevation of 1,700 feet. A carriage road leads from Breezy Point to North Woodstock, and the Flume, Profile, and Deer Park hotels are within a day's drive. Fine fishing and hunting as can be found in New Hampshire in immediate vicinity. Rates $3.00 per day. Special rates by week and month.

EDWARD B. WOODWORTH, Proprietor.

One person who came up every year and stayed for a week or more was Mr. Johnson of the Endicott Johnson Shoe Company. He made one trip up by stage that I doubt he ever forgot. Harry Fifield had a man who drove for him who was a tippler — he usually had a bottle with him — and he had charge of Mr. Johnson's stage on that trip. When they reached the South Peak and the ridge, they encountered a storm which I think was one of the worst of that summer. Mr. Johnson said that by that time the driver was useless, and he had visions of being blown off the ridge. Thanks to the sagacity of the horses they made it safely to the house and the kitchen door. Mr. Johnson was damn glad to reach the house. The driver wasn't even able to dismount by himself, and we had to take care of his team.

I think that some of the people who made extended stays of a week or more did so because of the undisturbed solitude that the mountaintop offered. People such as the two women from Shippens College and Mr. Johnson, who must have had weighty problems to consider, could mull over their difficulties and reach conclusions without any outside disturbance. They would spend hours at a time alone in sheltered spots on the peak, and they usually tried to avoid other people. I can recall one occasion when Mr. Johnson requested to dine with us in the kitchen rather than to encounter some people who were in the dining room.

Automobiles were not very plentiful at that time. My parents had friends from Worcester by the name of Griswold who started driving up the stage road in a Stanley Steamer. They were able to drive about half a mile before they had to leave it. I remember going down the mountain with them when they returned home and watching them get away in the car. A car was a novelty to us in those days.

There were days when we would have a lot of people at the summit, and some nights we were filled to capacity. Our most numerous clientele were the young people from the summer camps that were scattered around the lakes of the area. They used the house as an overnight stop on their hikes through the mountains. The nearby camps were those at Lake Tarleton, Armington and Baker ponds, Newfound Lake, and others, but we also were visited by camps from all over New England. There were a lot of camps.

People came from about every state in the country, and the mountain attracted many people from the local area such as Woodsville, Newbury, Hanover, and Bradford. Moosilauke, with the house perched on its peak had, and of course still has, a high degree of visibility for miles around, particularly from the

The Parker House was located along the Benton trail
at the northern foot of mountain.

Connecticut River valley and its foothills. To those who
had a view of the Tip Top House for the 365 days of
the year it acted as sort of a magnet. People responded
by making an excursion to its summit an annual event.
My parents were well known throughout the area, and
some people came up to visit and to "deadhead." One
of the first things they wanted was a pair of field glasses
so they could see how their place looked from the summit. Some of the residents in the valley felt that Moosilauke affected the climate, and there used to be a saying
in the area which I recall went something like this: "It
won't warm up and crops won't grow till Moosilauke
is free of snow."

Some hikers came up the north side of the mountain. There was a place on Tunnel Brook road owned by
a person named Lebina Parker which was named the
Parker House. It was little more than a bed and breakfast place, but it had enough guests to enable them to
keep busy during the summer and the hunting season.
It was the only house on that road that ran through the
valley from Glencliff to Wildwood.

We had two girls — a high school girl, Ora Lavoie, and an older person, Ina House — to help my mother with the kitchen and the housekeeping. The place would take care of forty or fifty people easily — more than that and it would get tight. We were always uncertain of the number of guests we would have — it might be five or fifty — and my mother had to be very versatile. A majority of the hikers used either the carriage road or the Glencliff trail. The two converged at the South Peak and then followed the bare ridge and the cone to the house. When hikers first came into view on the ridge, they were about an hour from the house, and my mother made everyone keep a hawk's eye on that ridge and count the people as they came over it.

There were times early in the season and during storms when we would be alone or have but few guests. My mother and her helpers would pass the time by making balsam pillows to sell in the office. There was a lot of ground balsam at the edge of the timber line which I would gather to provide the stuffing for the pillows. Its needles are very fragrant — at times their fragrance permeates the air. In the late 1960's, when I made a visit to the summit, I toted a big load of fir boughs down the Beaver Brook trail on my back. My youngest son, Larry, was with me, and I guess he thought I was crazy. Today the aroma of fir balsam makes me homesick for the mountain.

My mother and her helpers took advantage of every fine day to do the laundry. The clothes wouldn't dry when we were in the clouds, and on sunny days the area near the house looked like a patchwork quilt. The laundry could not be hung up to dry for the wind would blow it away or tatter it. The only way clothes could be dried was by laying them flat on the cranberry bushes and the ground balsam that dotted the peak. The wind never bothered them there, and it dried them quickly.

We obtained our drinking water from a spring that was just under the cone on the east side of the peak. It was about twenty-five or thirty rods down to it. Water was carried up to the house in two large sap pails hung from a sap yoke, and it was used sparingly for drinking and cooking purposes. There were occasions when the wind prevented us from getting any.

The wind often blows hard enough up there so that one can lean on it and be blown backwards at a rapid rate of speed. I can recall seeing my father come up onto the peak with two heavy pails of water hooked to a sap yoke that was balanced across his shoulders when the wind blew him, pails, sap yoke, and water halfway down to the barn. If swearing could have tempered the wind we would have been becalmed for the rest of the summer.

The mountain is abundant with springs which are close to its top. One of them is the headwaters of Gorge Brook. The source of their crystal treasure is a mystery. The headwaters of Baker River which flows southeasterly and becomes part of the Merrimack and those of the Wild Ammonoosuc and the Oliverian which flow westerly to the Connecticut originate near the top of the mountain and are quite close to each other. The spring nearest the top went dry one summer, and we had to use another that was about one-half mile from the house. Water for purposes other than drinking and cooking was piped into the house from large wooden tanks that were set under the eaves. They were lined with zinc, and they caught and held rain water and condensation from the clouds which often enveloped the peak.

The springs were icy cold, and we used to keep food in them. They were our refrigerator. Cooked food such as stews and casseroles would keep quite a few days. We didn't have much fresh meat. The stage would

occasionally bring up a quarter of beef, which had to be used quickly. Smoked hams and shoulders, bacon and eggs would keep for a long time, and staples such as flour, sugar, crackers, etc., we stored by the barrel. The buckboard trip up the mountain was so rough in spots that eggs had to be handled carefully to prevent them from breaking. The first year we were on the mountain my father tried keeping some hens, but they didn't stay around long. Unless they were kept shut in all of the time the wind would blow them down into Jobildunk.

The food supply problems limited our menu to simple home cooking, but my mother was a good cook, and the meals that she served gave the house a reputation for its cuisine. She made good doughnuts, about which there is an amusing story. That was the age of the Bloomer Girls, when the girls from the camps wore big baggy bloomers: each bloomer leg would hold a bushel. One night we had a troop from a girls' camp, and the next morning at breakfast my mother served her usual ample supply of doughnuts — platters of them. The girls made short work of them and began to call for more. My father kept an eye on them and discovered that the girls were stuffing them down their bloomer legs. He went into the dining room and approached the counselor, telling her in a loud, emphatic tone:

"We guarantee to fill your stomachs here, but I'm damned if I am going to fill those bloomer legs!" An extra charge for doughnuts appeared on her bill.

Another incident which was not so amusing at the time — at least not to my mother — occurred one evening at dinner. Many will recognize it as an old saw which they may have heard under different circumstances. In spite of that fact, however, I am including it for it actually did happen to us. It was accidental and uncomplimentary; not at all in accord with my mother's usual tidiness around the kitchen. She would be strongly against its being known, but after the passage of eighty years it can be related. One evening my mother had tomato soup on the menu; a kettle of it was simmering on the stove. Cooking at an altitude of five

Mabel Morse

thousand feet is tricky: things come to a boil quickly. Just as the guests were sitting down for dinner the soup suddenly erupted and boiled over. Someone shouted, and Ina, who was quite facetious, yelled, "Spit in it!" My father, who occasionally chewed tobacco, was doing so at the time and he tamed the soup with a generous amount of tobacco juice. My mother was furious, but there was hardly anything that she could do. The guests were at the table. Tomato soup was on the menu, and, with a high degree of apprehension, it was served. The results were unexpected. We had a run on tomato soup, with many requesting a second helping and giving my mother high praise, claiming that it was the best soup they had ever tasted. My father was partially exonerated, and my mother learned to add something to her soups to make them zestful — but be assured that it was something besides tobacco juice!

We were self-sufficient in one respect. We had a cow that gave us fresh milk and cream. Her name was Dinah. She was white with black spots. She was a big attraction to the guests, and had a write up in the old Boston Post. We leased her from an "Uncle Lee" Collins who lived in Benton, and she came up the Benton trail

Dinah the Cow at the kitchen door

every spring. As mentioned, the Parker House was at the foot of the mountain on Tunnel Brook. The Benton trail started there, and it offered the easiest ascent to the summit. The first year that we ran the house Uncle Lee delivered the cow himself, and his trip is well described by Theda Page Brigham in *More about Coventry–Benton* (1964). Theda was the small assistant who accompanied Collins, and was at that time, as she used to say, "young and full of beans." She wrote:

> *"Uncle Lee" hitched old Ben into the wagon shafts, tucked the noonday lunch under the seat, hitched the cow's halter to the tail of the wagon, patted his pocket to be sure he had the little mirror, and he and his young helper were off. Old Ben, wagon, cow, moved slowly out the east road, using up a considerable part of the morning in getting to Tunnel Brook. "Uncle Lee" tied old Ben in the Parker House carriage shed, hung a feedbag under his nose, and with axe in hand headed up the north trail. There were many "blow-downs" on the trail and he chopped a path while his small assistant led the cow, or prodded her. Anyone acquainted with cows will believe that she didn't climb Moosilauke of her own accord. She was pulled and urged. It was a long, slow ascent but the weather on the mountain was crystal-clear, the view magnificent, and the little mirror flashed the message of arrival down to Benton Street. Without the cow, the descent looked easy. It was, until the deluge came. The Thunder God pulled out all the stops, the little people in charge of rain emptied all their buckets! The trail was slipperier than a greased pig, the cowhands soaking wet. And that ornery cow was in a nice, dry stable on the summit!"*

There was a fair-sized barn below the north side of the cone where Dinah stayed in bad weather and at night. The stage horses were kept there whenever the stage stayed overnight, and there were some camps that

Dinah on the rocks

came up on saddle horses occasionally, so the cow often had company. We had a bell on Dinah, and she would come to the kitchen door and ring that bell until we brought something out for her to eat. She was the only cow I ever saw that ate garbage. She did most of her grazing on the east peak where the sparse growth was stunted, and there were quite a few open areas that were grassy. She was a good cow and ran loose on the mountaintop for the three summers that we were there without once offering to leave. Each fall we would coax her down the mountain and leave her with Lebina who would take care of her until Uncle Lee came to take her home.

The house and the roofs were anchored to the mountaintop by thick iron rods attached to eye bolts sunk in the ledges on the peak. The rods were round and about one inch in diameter. They were not very long, and it took at least two lengths, and sometimes three, joined together to form one tie-down. The rods were joined together by eyes formed in the ends, which created a slack and some play in the rods. During severe windstorms the wind would literally pick the house up until the slack in the rods was taken up and the building would then be rudely and jarringly jerked back to earth. It was a hairy sensation to lie in bed at night and feel the house move up and down with the wind. Lucy Larcom wrote that she actually became seasick in one storm that she experienced. We often wondered if the rods were going to hold or if the house and everyone in it would be blown off the mountain. The rods were effective, however, for the house stayed put until it was destroyed by lightning years later.

We experienced but one thunderstorm during the three years that we were on the mountain. The storms were always below us; they followed the river valleys. It was an awe-inspiring sight to look down on the thunderclouds and see the lightning playing among them hundreds of feet below. In those days the thunderstorms caused a surprising number of fires. I suppose that they were barns we saw burning, for at that time the area consisted mostly of farms, many of which were subsistence farms.

The one thunderstorm that we were in was a startling experience. Storms had been around us during the evening, and they must have met on the mountaintop after we had retired. There was one blinding bolt of lightning and a tremendous clap of thunder that shook the house and roused us out of bed. We grabbed clothes and blankets and emptied the house damn quick. We felt sure that the house had been hit. Fortunately, it had struck elsewhere on the mountaintop.

From our high point we could watch the storms building up on the far horizons and observe them traveling towards us — sometimes at amazing speed. Those that formed in the southeast over the Atlantic Ocean and that traveled our way to hit us seemed to be the most violent ones. Many of our guests came to enjoy

the view, and if we happened to be in a storm and
enveloped in clouds they would stay until the clouds
lifted. There were plenty of periods when we were
shut in by clouds, sometimes for several days to a
week. Often visibility would be no more than fifty feet.
There were times when we were alone in such storms.

Sometimes the clouds would settle down upon us
without a whisper of a breeze, and would envelop the
peak in a gray and dismal wraith-like silence. At other
times they would race across the mountaintop driven
by violent winds that howled and shrieked and rattled
the rods that held the house down. Late afternoons on
such dark and stormy days we would ring a bell or
fire some shots from a forty-five to guide anyone who
might be lost or confused by the storm. On several
occasions my father and I traveled the trails in search
of lost hikers. After being in the clouds for several
days it was a welcome sight when the sun would break
through and we could get a glimpse of the world below.

I recall one time in particular when we had been
in a storm for several days. It was late in the afternoon,
and the cloud that enveloped us was so dark that we
had to have lamps lit. We happened to be alone, and

were sitting in the kitchen when we heard a terrible
scream. It came from the office, and we found a woman
there who was prostrate on the floor just inside the
door. She was in a terrible mess, sobbing and over-
wrought. She had come up the Glencliff trail with four
or five girls and encountered the storm before they
reached the South Peak. They were afraid that they had
left the trail and were lost. She told the girls to stay put
and that she would try to find the house. She must have
had a terrible time. Luckily she hit the cone that goes
to the crest, but she did not see the house until she
bumped into it. My father and I went down the mountain until we found the rest of her party.

I remember another occasion when we had been
in a storm for about a week. Late one afternoon the
storm abated, and the clouds began to break up. There
was a thin wall of clouds off to the west towards Black
Mountain on which was portrayed a perfect picture. We
were looking on the shore of a lake as if we were within
a couple hundred feet of it. A boat with oars in it was
drawn up on the shore, and the features were distinct
enough so that the trees could be identified as white
birches. It was as if we were looking at a wide movie
screen. Of course it was a mirage reflected onto the
cloud by some freak of light, and I can envision it now.
It was one of the damnedest things that I ever saw.

Another time my father and I went down to
Glencliff to get some staples we needed: butter, salt, and
things like that. On our return up the mountain I had a
small pack on my back, and the one my father had must
have weighed 70 or 80 pounds. We hit the ridge, which
is just above timberline, at the same time that a vicious
storm did, and we literally crawled along it and up the
cone to the house.

The winds from Moosilauke travel far. There is
a phenomenon common to the Easton, Landaff, Benton,

and Bath areas known as the Bungay Jar. It often occurs in the fall, and both Theda Page Brigham and Ernest Poole attribute it to violent winds off Moosilauke that roar down through the Tunnel and Wild Ammonoosuc and up the Easton valley; a wind that howls, and is so strong that it jars houses as it hits. It is difficult to describe, but it is readily recognizable when it occurs. Old-timers used to call it the Bungay Bull or the Bungay Howl. Present day residents of any length of tenure call it the Bungay Jar. Wildwood was once known as Bungay, and the road westerly along the Wild Ammon-oosuc to Bath was called the Bungay Road.

We never had much of any problems with animals or patrons while we ran the house. There were quite a lot of rabbits around. My dog used to chase them, but there was never any chance of catching them. They would take refuge in the ground balsams which surround the bare peak. The shrubs were from two to three feet high with thick branches, and it was impossible to penetrate them. The very first night that we spent on the mountain we were awakened by a strange noise. There were small rocks piled in patio fashion around the house, and the noise sounded as though someone was dragging chains across them. My father

West & south sides with cables on the frame section

took a forty-five and went out to investigate and ran into a bunch of hedgehogs! They were quite plentiful on the mountain. They inhabited the stable where I suppose they were after salt. They gnawed away at both the stable and the house. We never saw any large animals on the peak.

I can recall but one time when my father was provoked by patrons. There was one group from Hanover — they might have been from Dartmouth — who came up to stay overnight. It was in the early years of the First World War before we had formally entered it. Late in the afternoon they had a meeting in the library. They told my father that they were going to have a prayer meeting and invited him to attend. He declined, saying that he could listen to them from the office. He listened, and found out that they were sympathizers with Germany. They were friends of the Kaiser, and they were praying for him. My father was patriotic, and at times he was quick-tempered. He kicked them out. He returned their money and told them to get the hell off the mountain — he wouldn't even give them anything to eat. It was quite late in the day, and they must have done some stumbling around in the dark before they reached the foot of the mountain.

Sunrises and sunsets were strong attractions to those who were enamored with the mountain. Many visited the peak for the express purpose of viewing them, and were very disappointed if the weather did not allow them to do so. Some would stay and ride out a storm for several days until the clouds lifted and we could see the world around us. On the 4800 foot peak both events occur when the world below is practically in darkness. Sunsets are very colorful. Lake Champlain, over 100 miles to the west, is a shimmer of gold about the size of one's hand, and the Adirondacks beyond it are outlined against the setting sun. The darkness of the valleys below is speckled with the lights of the villages around the horizon. In those days of railroad travel the headlights of the locomotives could be followed as they rushed along the river valleys.

To those who have experienced its splendor, sunrise has to be the grandest spectacle that the mountain has to offer. It was my duty to rouse those who wished to see it, and during our years on the mountain I witnessed so many occurrences of the event that it is burned into my memory. One has to rise early for the show starts about 4:30. There is no description that can do it justice. One watches the sun rise over an ocean of clouds that is formed from fog that fills the river valleys below; an ocean that extends to the horizons with the tops of the higher peaks rising out of it as islands. Lucy Larcom put it most aptly when she wrote that sunrise is something only to be beheld and experienced; not to be related. The sun rises and sets in its final stages with an amazing speed which makes one realize how fast our planet is spinning. The grandeur of both events makes one feel pretty small and insignificant.

Sunrises and sunsets were a part of nature's clockwork that performed daily. One could wait out a storm with assurance that they could be observed when the weather cleared. There were other events that occurred haphazardly. One has to be at the right place at the right time to experience them, and the fact that we were living on the mountaintop gave us that privilege. On a few rare occasions we saw displays of the Northern Lights. They are about as indescribable as the sunrise. The sky on the northern horizon seems to be bursting with curtains and rockets of every color imaginable.

I suppose that the purity of the air at that altitude makes the stars and the sky take on a larger dimension than they have when observed at a lower elevation. On a clear night with a full moon many of the distant peaks are visible. On days when the peak is clear there is always a grand view, but the far horizons are often hazy. It takes a rare combination of weather and atmosphere to make them stand out sharply.

At that time the Tip Top House on Moosilauke was the only one of its kind. It could not be compared with the famous and luxurious hotels of the White Mountain area which were operated on a grand and magnificent scale. However, they were not on a

HOW TO REACH BREEZY POINT.

This turn-of-the-century map shows the relation of Moosilauke to other resort areas, such as Fabyans, and the network of well-traveled railroad routes.

mountaintop. The only other mountaintop house was
the one on Mt. Washington. It could be seen easily from
Moosilauke on a clear day. At that time it did not especially cater to overnight guests, as it was readily accessible by the cog railway, and I believe that our Tip Top
House offered more home-like hospitality. The old
house on Mt. Washington was destroyed by fire in 1915.
I can remember watching it burn from Moosilauke.

We would watch the train going up Mt. Washington. Of course we could not see the cars, but we could
see the puffs of smoke made by the engine as it as-
cended the mountain. A railroad up Moosilauke was
planned back in the nineteenth century and some pro-
motion of it was made, but it never got beyond the
planning stage. We often signaled to Mt. Washington
with a mirror by flashing the rays of the sun back to
whoever we were communicating with. Flashing was
a popular pastime in those days. I often exchanged
flashes with a girl friend in East Haverhill. We never
used any sort of code, but just signaled to each other.
Black Mountain of the Hogback range was just to the
west of us, and could be called one of Moosilauke's

doorsteps. It had a fire tower which was occupied by one of our friends, and we exchanged flashes with him quite often.

For overnight stays we could generally handle forty to fifty people, but at the time of the Illumination of the Mountains in 1916 we must have had close to one hundred people who came to stay and observe the event. The spectacle might have been planned by the Appalachian Mountain Club. Flares, rockets, and fireworks were distributed in great quantities among the most prominent peaks and were scheduled to be lighted and set off in the evening all at the same time. Some of the peaks had large bonfires. Nature cooperated with perfect weather, and the affair was a huge success with rockets, flares, and fires visible all over the horizon. From our vantage point the Presidential Range was outlined in fire and light, and all of the peaks on the northern and eastern horizons were illuminated. The outline of the mountains looked something like Brooklyn Bridge at night when viewed from a distance. It was a real spectacle.

Many flares must have been burned, for the entire Presidential, Franconia, Starr King, and Pilot ranges were lit up. One of the men who helped with our display was the stage driver tippler, and he was well illuminated. He helped us put on a grand show. We had a small bonfire. I worked hard and long to provide wood for it. The spectacle was well publicized, and we were overwhelmed with people. We were able to feed them, but some had to sleep in chairs and on the floor. They were all over the place.

It was quite a chore to close the house at the end of the season. We usually arranged things so that we were practically out of supplies — we'd stay until the food ran out, and then return to the farm. The bedding and linens were stored in chests. We did not leave any part of the building open in the off-season. People did not visit the summit in the winter in those days. We planned to run the hotel until early fall to take advantage of the foliage season as much as possible. Of course it depended on the weather which was usually cold: the water pipes froze, and we often had light snow.

Every opening, every window, every door had big, solid shutters that were bolted from the inside. We had to be certain that everything was closed as tight as possible, because the house must have been hit with some terrible storms in the winter. Some of the storms that we experienced during the summer months gave us concern for the safety of the house. Perched as it was on the very top of the peak and exposed to the wind and the elements on all sides, it must have received much worse buffetings in the winter months. The fact that it withstood the elements for so many years was a tribute to its staunchness. Each spring when we returned to re-open it, we found it little changed from the way we had left it the previous fall.

We were on the mountain through 1917. When the owner of the Moosilauke Inn (Breezy Point had been renamed) heard that the Tip Top House was going to be given to Dartmouth College, he was quite disturbed. He knew that my parents were trying to buy it, and he offered the idea of forming a corporation. However, the Woodworths, who were the major shareholders, became the sole owners, and the property passed to Dartmouth College. To the best of my knowledge, our three years on the mountain were the last years that the house was run as a hotel, regularly offering rooms and meals and accommodations for an extended stay to the public.

The Woodworths were farsighted. Their gift to Dartmouth College proved to be the best thing that could have been done for the Tip Top House and the mountain. It placed them under the protection and

management of the Dartmouth Outing Club (DOC),
which assured them of permanency and security. The
DOC continued operating the house as a hostel until it
was destroyed by fire in 1942.

The Dartmouth landholdings on Mt. Moosilauke
have been expanded by gifts and by purchases and now
cover much of the south and east sides of the mountain,
including the headwaters of the Baker River. National
Forest surrounds the Dartmouth land. As a result, the
mountain has been preserved as a pristine wilderness
area instead of being subjected to the depredations of
timber operators and developers.

After my parents' tenure, the Tip Top House was
operated in the summer months by hut masters who
were students at Dartmouth, beginning in 1920. They
offered food and shelter to those who visited the mountain and in a way continued providing the services
which my great grandfather helped start in 1860. The
record of their occupancy and of their experiences has
been told in accounts written by some of them and
one in particular, titled "Home On A Hill," by Landon
Rockwell, who was hut master in the early 1930's,
gives an excellent and detailed description of their
experiences and the problems which they encountered.

Tom Burack, Bill and Larry Morse, and Will Brown at the ruins of
the Moosilauke Tip Top House, June, 1995

The Tip Top House burned, probably destroyed by lightning, in 1942. I remember looking at the mountain one morning and was amazed to see that the house was gone. The top of the mountain was strangely bare.

In June of 1995, about ten weeks before my 91st birthday, the hut masters held a reunion at the Ravine Lodge and graciously invited me to attend. I was helicoptered to the top of the mountain, where I roamed and poked around the ruins of the house, and sat in a niche on the crest; a niche which I first occupied eighty years before.

It was an unforgettable day; one in which I experienced and felt the full thrust of what I believe is an old Indian proverb used by Kipling in his story of Kim: "He who goes to the Hills goes to his Mother."

The Moosilauke summit as it now appears at the end of the Carriage Road. The older stone Prospect House was on the right, with the base of the wooden addition to the left.

Summit Ruins

This 1973 aerial view from the north shows the rectangular stony walls of the Prospect House (right) and the remnants of the first stable (center) at the end of the well-cairned Benton trail. Also present is the metal-sheathed Summit Cabin (1957–1979) maintained by the Dartmouth Outing Club, which provided mainly emergency shelter.

Forest
Years

Introduction to Forest Years

One of the great changes in America is the passing of the colorful individuals that once were a part of our country life. Men who were born into and raised in a different way of life. Men who could, and did, remember what life was like before electric lights, flush toilets, flying machines, TV's, and all the conveniences we today take for granted.

It is a sad fact that few of these colorful people still walk among us. "Old-timers," if you wish, who knew the hard life, hard work, and what it was like to earn a living by the sweat of brow and strength of muscle.

Another sad fact is that we have not taken the time to listen to these old-timers, to ask them questions, and to record what they had to offer. In a very few cases some of these old-timers did themselves what most of us failed to do — write their own story. Such a man is William S. Morse.

Bill Morse, who indeed can be called an "old-timer," has provided history with a look at the past through the following nine short stories he has called "Forest Years." Travel with Mr. Morse back into a past few readers can relate to. Read about the days when he was "full of beans" and crossed trails with some interesting people and knew interesting places.

Meet Ai, an old poacher who was trailed by the local Game Warden, a character himself. Backwoods encounters he tells about don't happen anymore.

He writes about the Big Wind of '38 when things were blown to "Hell and gone." And of the great amount of timber that was felled, and how it was salvaged, and of the men he calls "Watermen" who played a vital role.

His yarns about bears, backwoods camps, loggers, and "Old Pud" the Jobber, take the reader back in time to a way of life in the woods that will never return.

He recalls what the men were like in those days, where they came from, their nationalities, and what a haircut was like in Pittsburg fifty years ago.

Forest Years is to become a classic as time goes on. Thanks to an "old-timer" the past has been put into words, and print, for future generations to enjoy.

Paul Doherty
Gorham Hill, New Hampshire

(Paul T. Doherty is known throughout the North Country as a woodsman and great outdoors writer. He is the author of *Smoke From A Thousand Campfires*.)

Ai

In the late 1920's and the early 1930's, when I was young and full of beans, as one of my distant relatives used to say, I became tangled up with a person whose name was Ai. It was a strange association because Ai was described by the local citizens as one who was not quite "all there." Nature had not been very indulgent with him when she created his reasoning apparatus, but she made up for the omission by endowing him with an extraordinary insight into the way of the wilds and its inhabitants.

Ai had many talents which were only apparent when one accompanied him hunting or fishing or traveling the woods, a place he considered his particular domain. He seemed to have some special insight that made him privy to the thought processes and habits of animals. If he jumped a deer, he never bothered to trail it. He knew the exact place that the deer was headed for, and if he was low on venison he would hasten there to waylay it. He had a knack of knowing what days fish would bite, and there were people who regulated their fishing expeditions according to his actions. It was said that Ai could outrun a deer or smell a game warden a mile away. In addition to being simpleminded, he had many of the attributes of an outlaw.

Ai is an odd name, pronounced exactly as it is spelt — A-EYE. It was probably lifted from the Bible, as there was once a biblical kingdom or city named Ai. I have only encountered the name two other times during my life. When I was engaged in salvaging timber that was felled by the 1938 hurricane, we employed a lumber grader whose name was Ai Carr. Our work was done under the jurisdiction of the U.S. Forest Service, and we had to furnish the government with an extensive dossier on the key people we hired. When Carr's dossier reached Washington on its travels, they returned it saying that we had made an error in recording his name; they required a person's full first and middle name instead of his initials, and requested that we return a corrected dossier. We replied that Ai was his first name and that he had no middle name. The explanation did not satisfy them, and they made him furnish them with a birth certificate. There was also an Ai Otis Gould who dabbled in real estate in years past, and I encountered his name while making deed searches.

Ai was fortunate in not having to be very concerned with the mundane cares of the world. He did not toil nor did he spin. His father had left him a place that consisted of a few acres and a small house situated on a branch of the Gale River. His affairs were administered by an understanding guardian who managed to keep the property out of the hands of the tax collector, and Ai was free to roam the woods as he pleased. His only concession to any laws was to obtain a hunting and fishing license. Outside of that he followed his own rules. It was always open season on fish and game as far as he was concerned. He lived mostly on fish and venison, and he was a subject of concern to the game warden, who knew what Ai was doing. The warden labored hard to bring him to bay, but Ai was like a will-o'-the-wisp who managed to elude and tantalize him with a wry sense of humor.

I first ran into Ai one day when I was reconnoitering the Bog Pond area, a huge bowl that lies south of

156

Indian Head and the Kinsman range in the Franconia area of the White Mountains. I think that he had been watching me for some time trying to determine what I was doing. When he decided that I could not be a game warden, he made his appearance. I had a staff compass and a small plotting table both of which were foreign to him, and he was curious. It was evident that he had a few loose ends, and it took a little patience to explain my work. When he realized that I was attempting to draw a picture showing some of the features of the area, he became enthusiastic and began telling me things about that piece of country that would have taken me two or three days to ferret out. I learned that he had explored the White Mountain region from the Kilkennies to Mad River and that he was a living encyclopedia about its features in which I was interested.

I consulted him often, and hired him on occasions when I needed someone to work with me. I was the only one besides the wardens who ever showed any interest in his information or paid more than passing attention to him. He became sort of an appendage to me for a while, and a loose attachment was formed between us. Undoubtedly there were people who began to think that I was as queer as Ai.

My first inkling of any rift between Ai and the game warden occurred one day when we were fishing the Connecticut River. We were working in Dalton at the time, and a heavy shower had driven us out of the woods. It was early in the afternoon, and Ai reasoned that we had time to catch a mess of pickerel for supper. We were close to the mouth of John's River where it emptied into the Connecticut, and Ai said it was a good place to fish for them. The road at that time was within a few rods of the river, and we had just about wet our lines when the game warden drove up and stopped.

The warden of that area was a person who might as well be called Old Gil. He was an intimidating figure.

He was tall and big around, not exactly pot-gutted, but well padded around his waist, which was always adorned with a gun belt and holster that contained a Colt Forty-five. He had big feet and wore high boots that must have been at least size 12. I never saw him in a uniform; his only evidence of his authority was a badge. He always wore old clothes and looked as though he had been rolled down hill.

When he got out of the car I remarked that we had company, and as he approached us I reached for my wallet and started pulling out my fishing license. Gil looked at me and said, "Never mind, I don't care about you.

That's the Son of a B. I want," and he pointed to Ai, asking to see his license. Ai produced his license, handed it over to the warden, and said: "Here it is you pot-bellied old Bastid!"

Gil looked at the license, handed it back to Ai, got in his car and drove off without saying another word. Their conversation was not one that could be called very endearing, and I was uncertain as to whether their name calling was serious or meant to be in jest. I asked Ai about it, and he remarked that Old Gil didn't like him.

There was a war being waged between the warden and Ai. Gil was pursuing it seriously and aggressively. Ai was just as serious about it, but he injected a bit of humor into the fray. He told me about an incident that had happened a couple of years before. Ai was exploring the woods on one of the branches of Israel's River and found a stretch that looked promising enough to fish. He cut a pole, tied a hook and line on the end of it, and started fishing. Ai never burdened himself with a fish rod when he was roaming the woods. He carried a line and some hooks and would cut a pole when he wanted to fish. An alder pole and a short line makes a pretty handy rig on a brushy mountain stream.

Ai had been fishing a few minutes without any luck when he spotted Gil coming up the brook. Ai waited until Gil came close enough to see him. He threw his pole into the brush and started running through the woods with the warden after him. Ai said that he picked the roughest going he could find and that he ran just fast enough so that Gil could keep him in sight. When he saw that Gil was beginning to tire he stopped running and sat down on a stone. Gil came puffing up and demanded Ai's license which he readily produced. Gil then asked to see any fish that he had caught and Ai told him that he hadn't caught any, and that he didn't think there were any fish that high up in the brook.

"What the Hell were you running for?" Gil asked.

Ai replied that he was curious as to just how far

159

Gil could run before getting pooped. Gil didn't appreciate the joke.

Another time Ai was fishing the river near his house. He had a chowder in mind for his supper, and he was putting everything he caught regardless of its size into his creel. He was about ready to stop fishing and go home when Gil hailed him from the bank. He had been watching Ai for some time and knew that he had a creel full of short fish. His exuberance caused him to be hasty. "I've got you this time, Ai!" he yelled, "Let me see your fish." Ai, who was still in the stream, turned his creel upside down and dumped all of his fish into the river.

"There they are," he said. "Look them over."

Gil hopped up and down on the bank watching his evidence float downstream, and Ai went home to a fishless supper. He may have been simpleminded, but he knew that evidence in the brook could not be used against him.

Ai was not really a bad sort of outlaw. He was not hoggish, and his depredations did not amount to much. He only took what he felt he needed, and he did not resort to salting deer or to jacking them as many did. Compared to others at that time his trespasses against the laws were very mild.

The Depression was beginning to make itself felt, and there was considerable outlawry taking place. No one shied away from any chance to pick up a little money. When the weather was cold enough to freeze deer carcasses, some people smuggled venison to the cities. Many were caught jacking deer in wholesale lots, and there were some who experienced mishaps while transporting them. A lot of Christmas trees from the north country went to the New York market and a lot of venison went along with them. That was years before the Interstates were even thought of. The main route to New York followed the Connecticut River and went through the towns and villages that were along its banks. It wound through the heart of White River Junction where it went through a railroad underpass which had a very low clearance. On one occasion a truck load of Christmas trees went through it that was piled too high. The top layers of trees were shaved off creating a mess and a traffic tie up. When the police arrived at the scene they found the truck driver frantically trying to hide the carcasses of a number of deer that had been uncovered. They were probably worth more in the city market than his entire load of trees.

The era provided its humorous aspects. A friend who was a prominent judge told me of a deerjacking case that came before him. The warden presented his evidence against the culprit, going into some detail as to how he had caught the deerjacker. Both the judge and the warden came from the north country and had grown up as boyhood friends. The judge said that the only thoughts that went through his mind during the hearing were of the times that he and the warden used to jack deer together in the same manner. He knew damn well the same thoughts were going through the warden's mind, and neither of them dared to look at the other, for fear of bursting out in laughter. He said he gave the deerjacker as light a fine as he possibly could.

To get back to Ai, the only illegal thing that he introduced me to was bottle fishing. If you take a few fairly small empty bottles, cork them tightly so that they will remain buoyant, tie a fish line with baited hooks around their necks, and throw them into a pond you will have some fun. If there are any fish in the pond you will be busy chasing bottles all over the place. A buoyant bottle offers quite a bit of resistance to a fish. They get tired and have to stop and rest. Just as you reach out to capture a quiet bottle the fish comes to life again and you have to resume your pursuit of it.

Bottle fishing is an illegal procedure, and it gets so boisterous that it cannot be pursued quietly. There were only a couple of remote ponds where Ai felt safe doing it. They were too far back for boats, but Ai had rigged up an apology for a raft at each one, and he fished them occasionally. His rafts were scary things, but he did fine with them. I didn't dare go out on one, but it was fun watching Ai chasing bottles. It would probably be best to make it clear that bottle fishing is illegal and it should not be done. Any one caught doing it would probably have the book thrown at him.

When I became fully engaged in logging, I lost track of Ai, and I do not know how he made it through life or what became of him. He still comes to mind occasionally, especially when I browse through the fishing section of a sporting goods store and look at the many contraptions and lures that are meant to separate a man from his money. I think of Ai and the messes of fish that he caught with his alder rods, and recall his comment on such tempting lures: "Them damn things scare more fish than they catch."

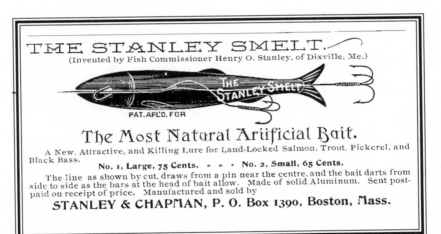

Big Wind

The custom of giving names to hurricanes did not start until around 1950, so the one of 1938 that visited coastal and inland New England was nameless. It was a doozie that blew steeples off of churches, damaged lighthouses, reduced homes to masses of kindling, caused hundreds of deaths, and injured thousands of people. Property damage was estimated at over one billion pre-inflated dollars, and it rampaged as far north as Lake Champlain which, according to one report, resembled the stormy Atlantic.

The storm was not unheralded, but like most such storms it was elusive and unpredictable. It had been skipping around the Caribbean and the South Atlantic for several days, changing direction quite often. At that time the modern communication and storm-warning system that exists today was unknown. Most reports of the storms came from ships that encountered them at sea. The storm had progressed without hitting the usual targets along the southeast coast, and it was not considered to be a threat, especially in New England, where such storms seldom occurred. In the afternoon of September 21st, practically without warning, it suddenly hit New York City and Long Island as a full-fledged hurricane that took lives, and destroyed thousands of homes, autos, boats, and other property along the coastal waterfront as it raged along the coasts of Connecticut, Rhode Island, and Massachusetts. When it reached the mouth of the Connecticut River, the hurricane used the valley as a highway along which it traveled, raising havoc until it blew itself out around the Canadian line.

The wholesale destruction of houses and other property inland was not as extensive as that along the coast, mainly because it was not as thickly settled, but it laid thousands of acres of timber as flat as if it had been cut with a scythe. The storm had been preceded by a period of heavy rain that had saturated the ground, 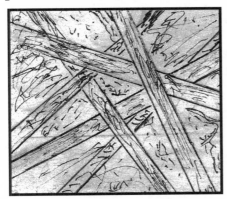 making the trees as vulnerable to the violent wind as the ten-pins in a bowling alley are to a well-thrown ball. The trees did not break off; they were simply uprooted and piled on top of each other like jackstraws.

The storm hit our area early in the evening, soon after our supper. Our three summers on Moosilauke had inured us to violent winds, but when we watched the shade trees that were in our front yard being uprooted and laid flat, it became evident that we were experiencing something unusual, and that it was unsafe to go outside. The wind had abated somewhat by the time we retired; no thought was given to any damage that might have occurred. It was not until we went outside the next morning that we realized we had been hit by a major disaster.

Our buildings were intact, but there were many structures throughout the countryside that suffered severe damage. The buildings of the farm that adjoined ours were a quarter of a mile away, and parts of the barn roof landed in one of our fields. The storm occurred at a time when the barns were full of hay which enabled their walls to stand, but many had their roofs blown off and scattered throughout the countryside — some of them landing upside down and resting on their ridgepoles.

A Mix of Years

One of our neighbors found his hen house and
hens missing, blown to Hell and gone; he never was
able to find any of them. Trees and downed power lines
barricaded the roads making travel almost impossible,
and as I recall, we were without power for three weeks
or more. The most apparent impact that the storm had
upon the countryside was in the changed appearance of
the surrounding horizon. Instead of the usual view of
trees and woodlands there was only a void; nothing but
empty space. We had a thirty acre stand of merchant-
able pine which my father considered to be one of his
prize possessions — better than money in the bank. It
was highly visible from our back door step. When we
went outside the morning after the big wind, that stand
of pine that had towered over the fields had vanished:
uprooted and blown completely flat. It was unbeliev-
able.

'38 Hurricane damage in
Jobildunc Ravine, Mt. Moosilauke
Benton, New Hampshire
J. Willcox Brown

At that time farms, both large and small, were dominant in New Hampshire and Vermont. The woodlots and their timber were valuable, and the cumulative damage that resulted from the wind was of some consequence. I was involved in logging then, and we were just getting started with the next winter's operations. Our plans and those of everyone else engaged in the industry suffered an abrupt change, practically coming to a standstill. The economic impact of the storm upon New England, which was struggling to emerge from the Depression, promised to be disturbing.

One of the greatest concerns in New Hampshire and Vermont and the river valley to the south was with the devastation of the timber, its effect upon market prices, and the fire hazard which was bound to occur. The Forest Service was assigned the responsibility of surveying the damage and coping with the problems that it created. I became involved in the project by first helping to assess the damage, and then serving as assistant supervisor in the salvage operations of the district that encompassed Grafton County and part of Sullivan County. At that time the area was quite heavily wooded with white pine predominating, and the Connecticut Valley and its foothills for miles each side of it had been heavily hit by the wind. There were individual areas of five thousand acres or more that were practically flat; areas of waste and desolation.

Roosevelt was fighting the Depression by opening up the Treasury of the United States, and a salvaging operation was formed that set up receiving sites where logs from the down timber were purchased at a fair market price. Sawmills were set up at the receiving sites, and the logs were processed into lumber. Receiving sites with mills were in operation within six weeks or so after the hurricane. Unless it is sawed into lumber and dried, white pine starts deteriorating quickly after it is cut. Logs came into the sites in such quantities that the mills could not handle them, and almost every available lake and pond in the area was used for storing logs to preserve them. Logs were landed on the banks of lakes and ponds and on the ice when the ponds froze over. They were boomed and stored in the water when the ice went out, and by the time a year had passed there were millions of feet of pine logs boomed in ponds throughout the area, where they were held until mills were set up to saw them out.

The same salvaging process was followed elsewhere in other counties and in Vermont, Massachusetts, and Connecticut. I have never known the final figure of the amount of timber that was salvaged throughout New England, but it must have been close to a billion feet. In our district alone we had ponds such as White-oak in Holderness and Post Pond in Lyme with four to six million feet of logs in each of them. Altogether we had about twenty pond and mill sites in our district where we received logs. After two years of salvaging timber I returned to logging and pulpwood operations, but most of the ponds remained to be sawed out when

Post Pond Hurricane Salvage
Lyme, New Hampshire

Scott Nichols

Gale River CCC Camp

I left. I have read that it took five years to salvage and saw out the hurricane timber in Connecticut.

There are places that still show the effect of the hurricane. Areas that were inaccessible or that did not contain enough pine to justify the cost of salvage were not harvested. The downed timber is now buried in new growth, and traveling through such places, scrambling over the uprooted trees that are now partially rotted, can be difficult.

The hurricane occurred at an opportune time to have some beneficial effect in northern New England. The Depression was still dominant, and many people were unemployed. The salvage operations created many jobs; jobs in the woods cutting and hauling out the logs. Conservation camps were set up, cutting out and establishing fire lanes, providing standby manpower and equipment to fight possible fires, and rehabilitating hard hit areas. Mills were set up providing work for many who were needed to operate them. Demand for scalers and lumber graders exceeded the supply, and men had to be trained for those jobs. The war in Europe began in 1939, and we were soon in a war economy. The salvage operation provided a large amount of lumber to meet its demands.

The hurricane of 1938 was an ill wind as far as the coastal areas of New England were concerned, but in spite of the damage that it did inland, it blew in some good to northern New England. The old sixteenth century quotation that it is an ill wind that blows nobody good proved to be true, and there were places and people who benefited from the disaster that was wrought by what was probably the worst wind that ever visited New England.

Boom Logs
Errol, New Hampshire

Paul Charest

Watermen

The hurricane of 1938 forced almost all woods operations of independent producers to practically come to a standstill until the damage was assessed and salvage procedures were initiated under the supervision of the Forest Service. Key men to oversee the job came from all parts of the country. The forester who organized Grafton and Coos counties came from the Coeur D'Alene in Idaho. Those counties were among the first districts in New Hampshire to become operational. I became his assistant, helping to set up and organize receiving sites, supervising the personnel involved in the operation: scalers, lumber graders, and the millworkers that sawed out the logs. It was work in which I had experience, but when the operation became

Driving pulpwood at Bean Brook
Berlin, New Hampshire, April, 1928

The Quarry Pile – softwood storage for winter use
Berlin, New Hampshire

involved in receiving logs at lake and pond sites and storing them there, I ran into something that was new and different to me. I became acquainted with men who could walk on water — provided they had a log under their feet.

The last drive of long logs that went down the Connecticut River occurred in 1915. By 1938 the only activity in our area making use of water transportation was that of the Brown Company, which was using the Androscoggin to drive four-foot pulpwood. Berlin was the only place in our vicinity where men could be found that knew water. The first two such men that were hired were engaged to select and prepare boom logs. As I recall, their names were Hubie Bolter and Whitey Bolduc; two men who at one time almost gave me heart failure.

A boom log has to be a pretty special sort of log, and we paid extra money for them. They are long and are made up by scarfing each end in a manner that squares it. The squared end is then bored with a hole to receive one end of a boom chain, by which the boom logs are connected to each other to create a pen which surrounds and contains an acre or more of floating logs. Making up boom logs requires good axemen, and both Whitey and Hubie were well qualified.

Boom Chain and Hook
Blaisdell Collection

Post Pond '38 Hurricane Salvage   Pauline Whittemore
Lyme, New Hampshire

The incident involving them occurred at Post Pond in Lyme, New Hampshire, where a large boom area was needed. Hubie and Whitey were building a pier to serve as a boom anchor. The pier was a large crib made of logs, built on the ice of the pond with the intention of sinking it after it was finished. It was filled with stones to give it weight, and it was heavy.

While Hubie and Whitey were capping the crib, using the polls of their axes to drive drift pins, the ice suddenly gave way and the pier went down with both men on it. There was probably twenty feet or more of water there, and my heart came up in my mouth, for I figured that they were lost. Their experience must have given them the presence of mind to do the only thing that helped save them. They hung onto the pier and rode it down until it hit bottom. When they let go, the pressure shot them back up through the hole in the ice as if they were propelled by a rocket, and we were able to pull them to safety. They were still holding their axes!

Although they didn't enjoy the plunge, they did not treat it as anything very unusual, and after that episode I have believed anything that I ever read or heard about rivermen and their exploits on the water.

When the boom logs were prepared, we had to have a full-fledged boom crew to place and maintain them and handle the logs while they were boomed in water storage. The man who had been hired as our boom boss was a person named Bill Hinchey, who came on the job with a picked crew from Berlin. I never saw Bill on a log, and I am not sure that he could ride one, but he had picked men who could, and they were a revelation to one who was not used to them.

A high bank above a pond was usually chosen as the yard for our receiving site. As soon as the logs were scaled they were rolled over the bank into the pond where they were floated out of the way. The procedure worked well in open water, but during the winter when the pond was frozen over the logs landed on the ice, and they built up into a snarled mass that was as high as the top of the bank. They stayed entangled along the shore even after the ice went out. The result was essentially a dry log jam twenty or more feet high that had to be unraveled by the boom crew.

Those men would go to the bottom of the jam underneath that high bank of logs and pry and pick away at them with peaveys until the jam loosened up at the bottom and hauled, spewing out a mess of logs which the men had to ride out into the pond. When the haul stopped, the men would return and start worrying at the jam again until they got another haul to ride out.

It was dangerous work, with a massive tangle of logs towering high above them that had the potential of violently collapsing at any time, calling for alertness and the ability to escape harm by speeding over a mass of floating logs on a second's notice. It was not as perilous as a whitewater river jam that had water pressure

175

Mill pond, crew, and Sawyer River Railroad (1915)
Livermore, New Hampshire
N.H. Hist. Society #F4458

behind it and fast water below it, but it was hazardous
enough to keep anyone who was watching the operation on edge. Those men could walk or run over a
bunch of floating logs as easily as if they were on solid
ground.

There was one man by name of Wes Farrell who
enjoyed standing on a single log, holding a peavey or a
pike pole, and riding it all over the pond. He was also a
wood butcher who made a headworks out of logs using
only his axe and an auger. A headworks is a raft with a
capstan, hewed out of part of a log, that is used to move
a boom by anchoring it and winding in the boom with a
rope. Wes was an old-timer, and he was an artisan with
an axe. I asked Hinchey about him, and he replied that
Wes was a good riverman in his day who, as Hinchey
expressed it, could ride a log down fast water like "the
Devil on a bicycle."

Hinchey was a big Bull-of-the-woods type of man
who affected an intimidating attitude that his large size

enabled him to get away with. A new supervisor came onto the job who was an exact opposite, and the two were not compatible. The supervisor fired Hinchey, who was no great loss, but he took his entire crew with him when he left, leaving us with about ten ponds full of logs and no boom crew.

We had a scaler from Maine who had been around, and I offered to make him boom boss if he could pick up some watermen. He left for Maine, and in a few days' time came back with two taxi loads of men who were veterans of driving Maine rivers — Bangor Tigers they were called. According to what I have read, there used to be considerable rivalry between them and the Connecticut River drivers in the heyday of the long log drives.

The Tigers were fully as good a gang as the Berlin bunch, and I became well acquainted with both crews. I am glad that I had the opportunity to do so, for they were part of a breed of men who have practically vanished in the limbos of time.

On the Androscoggin River
Berlin, New Hampshire
Peter Rowan
Northern Forest Heritage Park

Bears

The bear has been reputed to be the most powerful animal on our continent. Those who have seen his massive muscles after his skin has been removed, or who have witnessed the destruction one or more of them has done will not be inclined to dispute the fact. The black bears of the northeast are not as large as some of their species in other parts of the country, but they are powerful. They can kill an animal the size of a cow and walk off with it, or toss a log around as if it was a matchstick. People have been lulled into believing they are not dangerous because there are often times when they seem to be tolerant of humans. However, their tolerance is not a tolerance induced by lovableness and respect. It is a tolerance of disdain; the sort that some people show to those they consider inferior.

Bears were plentiful in our area when I was a kid. There was no closed season on them; they were a nuisance. Many of the farmers were unable to raise sheep because of the depredations that the bears made upon them, and my father once purchased an entire herd of cows from a farmer on the Stinson Lake road who stopped dairying because of the raids that the bears made on his livestock. They were hunted and trapped the year around because they were troublesome, and because a bearskin robe was a useful article. As I recall, there was a bounty on them at one time.

We had numerous minor encounters with bears while we logged in New Hampshire and Vermont, but it was when we moved into the Adirondacks that I became best acquainted with them. The Adirondack Park encompasses one of the largest wilderness areas of the Northeast, and we were in the heart of it. We soon found out that it was a habitat for bears; bears that were large and numerous and powerful. They were also sassy, and we had to live with them. Our headquarters in the Park was at Cedar River Flow which is on the Hudson River watershed, but our main camp and our biggest cut was about five miles west of there on Silver Run which is one of the headwaters of the St. Lawrence watershed.

The camp was built on a low terrace above the run, and we dug a large garbage pit about two hundred and fifty feet away at the foot of a large knoll on the opposite side of the run. We covered the pit by falling spruce trees across it. Those trees were large, as the entire area was virgin timber which had never seen an axe and but few human beings. We soon found out that the area in back of the knoll was a rather swampy tract that had become a bear wallow which was the home of a colony of bears. It didn't take long for them to take over the garbage pit. They threw aside the covering trees as though they were playing at jackstraws.

A one hundred and fifty man camp generates a lot of garbage, and the pit became a mecca to a bunch of bears every evening. They furnished amusement for the men, who would sit around the front of the camp watching them. After filling up on garbage, some of the bears were sassy enough to roam around the edges of the camp, and one had to keep alert, especially on a dark night, for he might run into one. They were tolerant, probably because they were too full of garbage to feel otherwise. We left them alone, and they did the same with us, but we never felt very easy with them around. They made it plain that we were the intruders.

Their activity began to be noised about the countryside. In spite of the fact that we were twenty miles back from civilization, much of which was over a damned poor road, people began to come on evenings

179

to watch the show, and they became a worse nuisance than the bears. We had to erect a gate at headquarters to keep them out. A reporter and a photographer from a paper in Utica, which was about one hundred and fifty miles away by road, came in for a story. They were zealous, and in spite of our admonitions they crossed the run and kept edging closer to the pit to get a picture. One old bear decided they were getting too close, and he suddenly turned and took after them. He chased the photographer and reporter back across the run and down the road. They made their shirt tails fly, and showed us that they were good sprinters. We were not bothered by them any more. I never saw their story or knew if they obtained any sort of a picture, but they gained some first hand knowledge about bears.

It requires a sizable crew to cook for and to feed one hundred and fifty men. We had a head cook, who had charge of several cooks and cookees. Our men were almost entirely French Canadians, and we had to have cooks who understood French cooking. They were always coming and going, and I had a standing order with our recruiter in Coaticook for a cook any time he could find one.

On one occasion a new cook came in with a taxi load of men. We were a long distance from Quebec, and they did not usually arrive at headquarters until late afternoon or evening. The next morning after the cook arrived the clerk at headquarters found him sitting on the office steps stating that he wanted to be returned to Canada; there were too damn many bears around our camp to suit him.

He and the clerk were arguing the matter when I arrived at the office. It was the first time that I saw the man. He was a typical French cook — large, well fed and padded, and leather-lunged. There was no need for a dinner horn or a gut iron to announce that it was meal time with them on the job. When one of them came to the door and bellowed, "Soupe!" everyone within a half mile of the place knew that grub was on the table.

The clerk and I tried to argue the man into staying, saying that the bears had never harmed anyone.

"Maybe not", the man said, "but last evening I had to go to the privy [he called it Le Cabinet] to take a dump, and after I finished I opened the door to leave, and a damned big bear was standing there. He was close enough so that the door hit him in his behind, and he growled at me."

"What did you do?" the clerk asked.

"By God, I shut the door and I sat down and dumped again!" he answered.

He was adamant about not staying, and we had to send him back by the next taxi that came down. We were required to post a five hundred dollar bond on each man, which was forfeited if he did not return to Canada. We had to return them if they didn't want to stay.

Some of the large paper companies such as International and Finch-Pruyn owned tracts of large acreage within the boundaries of the park. International owned a tract of several thousand acres on the headwaters and upper half of Squaw brook which they wanted us to cut while we were in the area. Squaw Brook empties into Cedar River several miles above the dam at the flow. It was an isolated area. The first time I went in to look it over I was accompanied by the head clerk, and we found that someone had been using the area, either to trap or to hunt. They had built a rough but quite comfortable camp beside the brook. It was a dugout type of shelter. They had dug down about four feet to create a small room which they lined with logs and over which they had pitched a tent. The only things inside the camp were the stove and the bunk frames. The other camp items, blankets, dishes, and food staples, had been packed in several heavy duty galvanized ash cans and hoisted up in the trees to keep them away from animals. No one had known that the camp was there, and the game warden decided that it belonged to a couple of outlaws who came into it by way of Speculator and Lewey Lake.

The next spring I went into the area with a jobber who was interested in cutting it. We intended to spend a couple of days cruising the job and planned to stay overnight at the outlaws' camp. After the first day of cruising we headed up the brook to the camp and found it to be a scene of utter destruction. It looked as if a bomb had hit the place. The tent was down and in shreds. The stove was smashed into bits, and the logs that lined the interior had been ripped down and scattered throughout the dugout. The bears had managed to get at the ash cans and they must have played ball with them. Their sides were stove in, the cans were crumpled up, and they looked as if they had been run over by a tractor. Ripped up blankets and broken dishes were strewn all over the place. The bears had left a strong message that intruders were unwelcome, and the jobber

lost any interest that he had in cutting the job. We never were able to find a jobber to cut it because of the bears, and we had to do the job by establishing our own camp. After we were in there and the garbage pit had been built, our experience with the bears was about the same as that at the main camp. Their use of the pit offered sort of an uneasy truce between us.

A bear is like a hog; he is always hungry, and will eat anything that a hog will eat. One of the cookees at our main camp had a tentative friendship with a hoary old bear that he called Joe. After supper the cookee would go out by the road with a kettle full of scraps, start banging on the kettle and yelling, "Come on Joe."

In a few minutes old Joe would come ambling out of the brush and start eating the slops. He was big and he was wary; he never took his eyes off of anyone who was around, and no one ever went very near him. He was old and gray in spots, and he probably didn't fare very well competing with the younger bears at the pit.

I have known people who have been in the woods all of their lives and never seen a bear. They are wily and cautious animals who ordinarily make it a point to avoid people. They are usually encountered when a person is quietly traveling alone. My early work in the woods mapping forest covers and also my later work surveying and cruising was often done alone, and I ran into bears on a number of occasions. None of the encounters were very eventful, but I did learn some things from them. If one is traveling with the wind so that the bear can get scent of him, they will seldom be seen. A bear has an odor of its own which is quite distinctive. It is not strong and long lasting like that of a skunk. It is elusive, and is sort of sweet and cloying. To me it smells something like sweet fern. If one is traveling with the wind and suddenly notices such an odor it means that a bear has been there a short time before, and that he vacated the area upon getting a scent. It is when one is traveling against the wind that they are suddenly encountered. In most such cases the bear is as startled as you are and will make the same haste in getting away. If he stops or rares up he is probably trying to figure out what you are. Like most large animals, his eyesight is much poorer than his acute sense of smell.

In any case, if you encounter one you had better get away from him as quickly and quietly as possible. It is not a good idea to run. It may lead him to chase you, and few people can outrun a bear. He is not a customer to fool around with. If you plan to do so, or

184

to hunt for them, you had better have a high-powered weapon and be a damned good shot.

The Vermont Panther or Catamount cannot be overlooked when writing about scary New England animals. At the time we were operating in Vermont its presence was a subject of some controversy. The last one shot in that state was in 1881, and for years there was no good evidence proving that any had been seen since that time. There were rumors, but except for a few people who claimed that they had seen one, they were considered to be extinct. I never saw one, but there were three incidents involving some of our men that convinced me that a few were still around. One involved a woods boss who had worked for us for some years. He had spent his life in the deep woods, and had seen about all that there was to be seen; he was not easily spooked. He came out of the Mt. Moses area one day and quit his job. He claimed he had seen a cat that had

CATAMOUNT MONUMENT.

a long tail and was much larger than a big dog. He said it was mean enough to switch its tail and snarl at him. I had to put him on a job in another area. There were two other separate instances, one in Chateauguay and one in Lakota, that involved two Canadian crews. They came out with all of their tools and quit a good chance where they were making money, because they had seen a similar animal. They were ready to leave without having their wood scaled. The fact that their actions were detrimental to them convinced me that they had seen something unusual that spooked them enough so that they didn't want to stay in Vermont. That was in the early 1940's, and I believe that enough evidence has been obtained recently to prove that the catamount is still roaming the woods of the state.

We had one other interesting and provoking experience with animals when we cut Corbin Park, a large private game preserve in New Hampshire. The preserve contains thousands of acres that are entirely surrounded by a strong, high, woven wire fence. As I recall there are about thirty miles of fence with a very few gates that offer access to the area. It is a hunting preserve that is stocked with various species of animals including elk and wild boar. At one time they had a number of bison in the park. I made my first acquaintance with the park at the time of the 1938 hurricane, when I was employed by the Forest Service helping to estimate the damage caused by the disaster.

The park was one of the first areas assigned to me, and an assistant and I first entered it early one morning by the north gate. It was an extremely foggy and misty morning in early October, and visibility was not much more than fifty feet. In rounding the point of a ridge we suddenly found ourselves in the midst of a herd of buffalo that were feeding in a small grassy meadow. A buffalo is a large animal, and in the fog and mist they loomed up as big as a house. Encountering

something as unexpected as a herd of buffalo in New Hampshire was a startling experience, and my assistant started hightailing back towards the gate with his shirt tail flying.

In the mid-1940's we purchased the spruce stumpage in the park and cut it for pulpwood. We soon learned that a wild boar can be worse to encounter than a bear. They are not as powerful, but they are more vicious and aggressive. They are possessed with curved, razor sharp tusks that can do a lot of damage. We had an unholy time keeping scalers on the job. The boars avoided the cutters as they were working more or less in company with others. Scalers worked alone, and a boar would almost invariably take after them, forcing them to take refuge on top of a pile of wood or up a tree. They were persistent, and would keep a scaler on top of a woodpile or up a tree for a couple of hours or more. On one occasion, during the winter, they forced a scaler to climb a tree when he was on snowshoes; an almost impossible stunt. "By God," the scaler said, "a man can do anything when one of those critters is after him!" The turnover of scalers was high while we were in the park.

According to the records of the early settlers, bears and panthers were plentiful in the north country, and they were a menace. The early settlers reared many swine which they allowed to run at large in the woods where they subsisted on roots and acorns and other nuts which were plentiful. Bears found them a good source of food, and their raids upon the herds were damaging. The settlers imported and raised large boars which ran with the herd to protect them, and there are reports of wild melees in which bears were killed by the boars.

I believe them. Both bears, which are indigenous to New England, and wild boars which are not, are dangerous animals. If I had to choose between unexpectedly running into a bear or a large wild boar in the woods, I think that I would opt to meet the bear, unless the bear happened to be a female with cubs. In that case it would be a toss-up.

Camps

Back in the days when a woods operation smelled of sweat and leather and horse manure instead of gasoline and diesel oil, logs and pulpwood were produced by men swinging axes and pulling crosscut saws and bucksaws. It probably took ten to twenty times as many men to produce the same amount of timber that can be produced today with the aid of chain saws and other mechanized equipment. According to some reports that I have read, chain saws are being replaced by machines that take down a tree by holding it while it is sheared at the stump and which then limbs it and cuts it into logs, all in one operation which is performed in a matter of minutes. Such production line processes come under the heading of progress, which is fine as long as we do not progress ourselves out of existence.

The changes wrought by the mechanization of logging operations have had about the same effect on the industry as the automobile had upon Old Dobbin.

It has been years since I have had anything to do with logging, and except for what I read, I am not familiar with present day procedures. From what I have observed a large amount of the timber cut in New England today is cut by men who commute daily from their homes to the woods. Logging camps, and the men who inhabited them, which were fairly common in the early decades of the twentieth century, seem to be mostly a thing of the past. In northern New England the large companies that own vast acreage may maintain a few camps, but most of them are probably serviced by gravel roads and are readily accessible to men who own a car and a chain saw or are heavy equipment owners and operators.

In my logging days few people owned autos, and a logging job was not reached as easily. Even on a small job a camp to house and feed the loggers was a necessity. Camps were built some distance back in the woods in the area to be cut, and they were serviced and reached by a tote road which usually was so rough and muddy that it could be traveled only by a horse or shank's mare. A few buildings were thrown together with cheap lumber and covered with tar paper. A camp built to service a fifteen or twenty man job created a small settlement occupying a clearing in the woods. The bunk house, sometimes known as the bar room, and the

cook shack, where the men ate, were usually separate buildings. In some camps they were connected by a structure called a dingle which served as a wash room. The horses were

Lumberman's Shanty

MANY a backwoodsman will recognize this picture of a lumberman's camp in the wilderness. No matter how poor the lumberman may be, and whatever his trials, and they are many,—whether he is known or unknown, rich or poor, in the lumber camp a stranger is made to feel at home. if worthy; if not, woe betide the weary traveller or wild woods tramp who seeks shelter beneath the hospitable roof of a chopper's dwelling.

From *Scribner's Lumber and Log Book* (1895)

housed in a barn known as the hovel. It was usually the largest building of the camp as horses and the hay and grain needed to feed them required a lot of space. A large job that called for quite a number of horses had a stableman to take care of them, and he usually bunked with them. The hovel also was home to a large colony of cats that played an important role in controlling the rats that came in with the grain in prolific numbers. At the conclusion of a job there were usually many more cats than horses occupying the hovel.

A shop, fully equipped with a forge and hand operated drills, held a supply of horse shoes, iron, logging chains, and other supplies that were necessary for the job. The shop was the domain of the blacksmith and another artisan known as a wood butcher — a man who could go into the woods with only an axe and an auger and build a pair of sleds that would survive the severe wracking that only a woods road could give them. Often both jobs were filled by one man. In addition there was the office, which housed a clerk; and the

Winter sledging (c. 1900)   E. Whitcher Collection
Warren, New Hampshire

wangan, which had an extra bunk for the scaler or any
outsider who had need to stay overnight. Last, but not
least, was the john, which was a four or five hole privy
located some distance from the rest of the camp and its
water supply.

    If there happened to be a sawmill on the job, its
crew maintained their own camps. In those days the
mill would be a portable one powered by a steam boiler.
A forty or fifty man job could result in quite a large and

busy settlement. The camp was not a place of luxury. It had a strong smell of wood smoke and horse manure, but it was a welcome place after one had spent several hours walking a job on a cold, windy, winter day. Thawing out in the cook shack while sipping a cup of hot tea or coffee that was strong enough to float nails on was a pleasant experience.

Each camp differed in its appearance and in the way it was run. The camp usually belonged to a jobber who had contracted to cut the job, and he was the lord of the manor. He usually owned the horses and equipment and had a following of men who worked for him and formed the nucleus of his crew. We walked his job often enough to make certain it was progressing according to agreement. Outside of that we had but little say in how he ran his operation. Each jobber ran his camp in his own way, and he was usually a pretty independent individual who handled and took care of his men as he saw fit.

The jobbers were a varied lot, and some of them had larceny in their souls. Their credit was not the best, and payment for all of their supplies and the money due the men became our responsibility. They were paid by us and charged to the jobber's account. We usually had a headquarters that was run by a head clerk in a location that enabled it to service several jobs and camps in its area. It was the focal point for receiving and distributing the men and supplies and for paying the men when they settled up and "went out."

The quality and amount of food served was one key factor in keeping a camp full of men; the food had to be the best, and it had to be plentiful. The jobbers charged the men between fifty cents and a dollar a day for board, depending on the price level for supplies. Most of the jobbers considered themselves lucky to break even on feeding the men.

There was one jobber known as "Old Pud," who often cut logs or pulpwood for us. Pud aimed to make a profit on his cook shack. His wife served as cook, and he did his best to keep the deer population under control. His men enjoyed the luxury of eating venison frequently. Every fall when he started a new job he brought in about a dozen young pigs that ran loose around the camp, while he fattened them up by feeding them the leftovers from the cook shack. During the winter months they furnished him excellent and inexpensive meat for the table. There was never any complaint from the men about the food at Pud's camp. However, the pigs could become a nuisance. When the nights became cold, they kept warm by burrowing in the manure pile at the hovel or by huddling together in front of the privy door, making the entrance to it a muddy and slippery mess which was hazardous to negotiate.

I happened to be staying at Pud's camp one cold fall night when one of the men woke up seized with an urgent need to visit the privy. The night was dark, and his pilgrimage was compelling. He rushed down the path, clad only in his underwear and rubbers, without thinking of the pigs. When he reached the privy door and stepped on them, they upended him, trampling and rolling him around in the mud. He accomplished his mission in an unexpected manner, and the squealing and swearing created an uproar that aroused the entire camp. The next morning after breakfast the man settled up and left camp. He shouldered his turkey and headed down the tote road vowing that he would never again ship into any damned camp that had a bunch of pigs running loose.

In those early years of the century a logging camp was a rough place that was inhabited by rough men. The bunkhouse was taken care of by a person who was

Old woods bunkhouse (c. 1900)   Paul Charest
"Amenities were scarce."

known as the Bull Cook. He kept the place clean, toted
in water and fire wood, and kept the home fires burning. He did his damnedest to keep the place free of
bugs, but he faced a losing battle. Bed bugs and body
lice were a fact of life in a logging camp, a fact that I
became aware of at an early age. When I was a kid, my
father operated logging jobs, and there were times when
he had to stay a night or two in the camp on the mountain. When he returned home after such a sojourn, my
mother would not let him in the house until he had
shed his clothes in the woodshed and put on some clean
ones. Some camps were quite notorious for their bugs,
but the men were inured to them and accepted them as
bedfellows. When a man came into camp he was given
a new tick and some clean blankets. He made a mattress
out of the tick by filling it with hay or straw from the
hovel. However, if he came from a flop house, he was
almost certain to have a few companions riding on him.

They breed fast, and it was impossible to keep a bunk-house free of such livestock.

Each individual camp had a short life; few of ours lasted more than a year. When the cut which they serviced had been completed, the camps were abandoned and became ghost towns. It did not take long for nature to obliterate them, bed bugs and all. On a large cut, such as we made in the Adirondacks, we used our main camp, which was a one hundred and fifty man camp, for four years, but during the last year it served mainly as a supply camp. When a job was cut and the camp broke up, the buildings were usually left, standing empty and forlorn until they succumbed to the ravages of nature and the new growth which rapidly began to appear.

Contrary to what seems to be popular belief, timber operators of my day did not ravage the woods. That was done before my time by the timber barons who pushed logging railroads into the heavily timbered areas and clear cut them. We cut what was ready to be cut, and left the balance for further growth. I have seen loads of logs being trucked out of the woods today that had to be cut from trees that the men would not have looked at sixty years ago. They would laugh at you if

you tried to get them to cut such timber — if it can be called that. Evidently the chain saws and the present day mechanical monsters which are capable of cutting acres in a day, combined with high prices, make it profitable to cut stuff that we would have left. From what I have been able to observe, I would say that we left the woods in much better shape for future generations than many do today.

Labor

Compared to today's requirements, doing business in the nineteen twenties and the thirties was relatively simple. At least it was in the woods industry, and I think the same was true of most other ventures. If today's entrepreneurs could realize the freedom of action that existed in those days, they would cry in their beer. We were not swamped with the costly paper work and regulations that are in force at the present time.

Our yearly production of logs and pulpwood was made up of the combined cuts made by a number of jobbers. Many of them were small jobs of a million feet or so of logs or one or two thousand cords of pulpwood. Unless a job was large enough to need a clerk, the jobber himself kept his own records in his own way, and probably he was the only one who could understand them. His records were about the only payroll records that were kept, and they consisted only of a man's scale that showed the amount of wood that he had cut and the board and wangan charges against him. Old Pud kept the records of his job by penciled notes jotted down in a ten cent notebook, which he kept under his pillow. In ten minutes' time he could tell you the scale of each man and the total cut of his job to date. He had a record of the total charges that we had against him, and he had a close idea of just how he stood — whether he was in the hole or had any money due him.

The records that we kept were about as simple. Everything was based upon piece work. Our contract with the companies for whom we were producing, our contracts with jobbers, and their payment to their men were based on a price of so much per cord or per thousand feet of logs. The loggers who actually cut the job

Above – Log-marking hammer
Large cant hook and peavey
Below – Felling or splitting wedge

A Few Logging Tools of the Trade
Edwin Blaisdell Collection, North Haverhill, N.H.

Above – pike pole
Caliper for measuring log length
Below – spud for peeling bark

were the low men on the totem pole, and were next door to being anonymous. They were working for the jobber, and their names appeared only on the scaler's tally sheet and in Pud's notebook. Last names were not important in those days; there were some who had no intention of giving their real names. There were no taxes or any other money to be withheld for the state or the government. Social Security and other similar things were in the future. A man's earnings were all his to do with as he pleased, and names were only a matter of record.

A logger was often known to his colleagues only by some name that was descriptive of his prowess or his habits. No one knew Bucksaw Sam's right name, as he went by several names. When Social Security cards became a requirement, Bucksaw had a half dozen cards, each with a different name and number. If you were seeking information about a person named John Allen, few would know who you were talking about if you used his full name, but you would get some response if you made it known that you were looking for Johnny B'Jesus.

The passage of the Social Security Act in 1935, which required us to withhold and pay a percentage of a man's earnings to the government, began the process of change and necessitated the keeping of some sort of

formal payroll records. The jobbers could not be entrusted to do it, so it became our responsibility. When we began withholding the money, the men did not believe us; they suspected that it was something we had cooked up to rook them with. When it became apparent to them that it was a law that everyone had to contend with, they were highly resentful of it. They suspected that it was a Ponzi scheme, and did their damnedest to avoid applying for a card and a number. When Social Security first went into effect, the employers had to apply for a card and a number for each man, who was supposed to furnish his birth date and other vital statistics. We had to battle with them to get the information, which they considered was no one's business but their own.

In 1938 the National Wage and Hour law was enacted, calling for a minimum wage and a forty hour week. The woods industry did not pay any attention to it as a decent logger earned much more than the minimum wage. The men all put in more than a forty hour week. A lot of them were daylight to dark men, and they were definitely not hourly workers. The Department of Labor, which did not know any more about a logging operation than a goose knows about God, took a different view. Around 1940 or 1941 they began to invade us with inspectors to see that we were complying with the law; an investigation which often took on a comic aspect.

When it became apparent to them that the men were working for the jobbers, they invaded the camps and the woods trying to explain the law and its ramifications to the jobbers and the lumberjacks and telling them what they had to do to comply with it — an approach that was not viewed with much enthusiasm by the men. The government men were from Boston and vicinity, dressed in the fashion of the city, and were an

Mt. Moosilauke loggers (c. 1900)   Marjorie S. Davis
East Warren, New Hampshire

incongruous sight traveling through the brush and mud
of a logging job in low dress shoes, a white shirt and tie,
coat and vest, and a homburg hat. They even tried to
sell the idea of installing a time clock in the camps. They
quickly provoked the jobbers to such an extent that they
refused to even talk with them. It was common practice
to feed any outsider who was around a camp at meal
time, but the jobbers drew the line on feeding those
"Bastards from Boston." They had to bring their own
lunch or go hungry.

The loggers were not at all cooperative with the
inspectors, and in spite of the fact that they were a
nuisance, there were occasions when I felt sorry for
them. They tried having evening sessions with the men
and talking with them in the bunkhouse after supper,
but they were usually hooted down. On a number of
occasions they were literally booted out of camp and
had to stumble their way down the tote road in the
dark. They would complain to me of the treatment they
received, thinking that I could do something about it.

I tried to explain to them that they were dealing with an independent breed of men with Yankee characteristics who could not be confined within rules that dictated anything they could or could not do; men who were of a different mold than the ones they were used to.

The inspectors finally realized that cutting logs and pulpwood could not be adapted to production line procedures. Their only success was with the cooks whose work necessitated that they put in long hours in the cook shack. They found one cook who put in a claim and received a settlement for overtime. Otherwise, the time which the inspectors spent on our operations was not very productive. However, it greatly increased the necessity that we keep more records.

In 1943 the bill calling for the withholding of income taxes from the men's earnings was passed. At that time the country was engaged in the World War, and a large number of lumberjacks had left the woods for the high paying jobs of the shipyards. We had to import most of our men from Canada. According to the agreement between the two governments, they were not subject to our withholding tax, but additional records and reports were required for the Americans that worked for us.

The arrangement that freed the Canadians from our tax seemed unfair, and the Americans who worked for us resented it. At one of our Vermont headquarters we had a small bunk house to take care of new men who arrived in the evening too late to send out to a camp. Often more men came in than we had bunks for. We had an old bull cook called "Freezie" who took care of things around headquarters, and I asked him if he had a hard time taking care of the excess men. "No trouble," said Freezie. "Them that pay the 'skin-come tax' get the bunks, and them that don't sleep on the floor." If that happened under today's rules, someone would probably sue us for discrimination, and the courts would probably uphold them and hit us for damages that would be ruinous.

When we moved into the Adirondacks, we began to get more federal rules and regulations and also some imposed by the state concerning the camps. One concession that we made in regard to the camps was the installation of a generator and electric lights at our main camp, which was a big change and improvement from the oil lamps and lanterns that had been used before. The regulations that we were encountering and those that we could foresee on the horizon were a big factor in our decision to stop logging. It is tough enough to buck the laws of economics without having to contend with those enacted by the state and federal legislatures. I feel sorry for those who have to do so today.

Haircut

The wildest haircut I ever got was one I received in Pittsburg, New Hampshire, over fifty years ago. The year was 1941. I was in charge of two hardwood logging jobs that we had going in the area. Tilton and St. Claire were cutting a million and a half on Perry Stream, and Old Pud was cutting a million feet on the height of land between Perry and Indian. Tilton's camp was on the west side of Perry Stream not very far upstream from Happy Corner. Pud's camp was on the height of land about opposite Chapple's camp on Indian. That was before the access road up Indian Stream was built, and we toted into Pud's camp from around Back Lake.

People who were closely involved with a logging operation did not have much concern with their appearance, and shaggy hair was commonplace. A lumberjack's work and his surroundings were bound to make him appear unkempt, but he was not a tramp. Many of them were family men who went home weekends when they could manage to do so. A logging camp in those days did not have any bathing or laundry facilities, but those who remained in camp for the weekend usually shaved and cleaned themselves up as much as possible while observing Sunday as a day of rest. Oftentimes there was someone in camp who cut hair as a sideline, but as a rule the men delayed such grooming until they went out, and they became pretty shaggy.

It had been a hectic winter with a lot of thawing weather that raised hell with moving logs, and we just barely got our cut out before break up. I was so absorbed in the jobs that I paid no attention to anything else. My wife and I had an apartment in Colebrook,

206

MAIN ST., PITTSBURG, N.H., 33.

Barber Shop
Pittsburg, New Hampshire

and on most days I managed to get home during the evening hours. I usually traveled the back road from Pittsburg to Colebrook through Clarksville, which to my mind is one of the most scenic areas in New Hampshire, especially on a glistening moonlit winter evening. Traveling it was the most relaxing period of my day.

I did not realize how unkempt I must have appeared until my wife, Lois, complained that I was so badly in need of a haircut that she was ashamed of me, and I promised that I would get one at the first opportunity. Not long after, when we began to see light at the end of the tunnel, Pud and I made a visit to the barbershop in Pittsburg. There was only one shop and one barber in town. It was on a Saturday afternoon and there were several customers ahead of us and we had to wait our turn.

Ever since its inception Pittsburg has been known as somewhat of a woolly place. It has the distinction of being one of the few places to secede from the United States, declaring itself to be an independent entity. It called itself the Indian Stream Republic and had a small army. For a few years during the 1830's, it had skirmishes with both New Hampshire and Canada.

It was still a woolly place when I got my haircut, and I found out that the barber shop was the sort of establishment that one should keep away from on a Saturday afternoon.

The shop had a back room that was frequently visited by those waiting their turn for a haircut, and the barber joined them between jobs. It didn't take long for the atmosphere to take on a jovial conviviality, and with each trip to the back room the barber became more boisterous in flourishing his shears. Whatever he was getting for nourishment in the back room had the same effect as feeding more gas to a chain saw. By the time he got around to me, he was more interested in talking than he was in cutting hair. The operation became sort of a hit or miss affair, and I became concerned for the safety of my ears.

I didn't remain to watch the barber work on Pud, and found out later that he closed up shop after finishing me off, telling everyone to go home and to come back Monday. I guess that it was a usual Saturday afternoon occurrence with him. Lois did not feel that the haircut made much improvement in my appearance. She used to work as a hair dresser, and tried to smooth off the rough edges that were plentiful.

That haircut that I had in Pittsburg was an event that happened a long time ago, but I still think of it and the barber whenever I climb into a barber's chair. I hope that Pittsburg is still as woolly as it was back in those days. It would be a shame for such individuality to disappear.

Men

During my time most of the logs and pulpwood that we produced were cut by men of French Canadian descent. They were the backbone of the woods industry in our area. There were many men of other nationalities, but the French Canadians were here before they came. There were numerous French families in our area. They formed a large part of the fabric of our countryside, and were as much a part of it as the descendants of the early settlers. I think that they first arrived to work cutting the wood that the railroad engines burned before they were converted to coal. Some of them remained and became a big factor in the economy and life of our area. Many of them bought farms and raised large families; others stayed to become part of the woods industry. They were hard workers. Many of them had grown up with an axe in their hands, and they knew the mechanics of logging as it was done in those days. As the paper mills expanded and the demand for pulpwood to feed their machines increased, more men came in from Canada. They were, for the most part, family men whose livelihood depended upon the woods.

The other nationalities such as the Swedes, Finns, and Norwegians arrived with the tide of immigration, and the Russian Revolution was responsible for an influx of Russians, Poles, and other Slavs. Most of them were homeless and bewildered in a strange land. Many of them had an agrarian background which made them adaptable to the woods, and the logging camps and flop houses became the only home that they knew. They were joined by drifters and by some who were running away from trouble. A camp comprised of men of French

Getting ready for...

Canadian descent or of Norwegians and Finns was
reasonably stable and predictable. A camp filled with
a polyglot mixture of drifters and different nationalities
was like a case of dynamite waiting for a fuse to be lit.

      The jobbers who contracted to cut a sizable job
usually had their own following of men, and our only
contact with the lumberjacks was processing them
through headquarters and distributing them to the
various jobs which we had going. Although they were
employed by the jobbers, they looked to us to guarantee
their pay. They were delivered to headquarters by taxis
owned by recruiters who serviced the woods industry.
Except for the family men, they almost invariably had
some sort of a tab against them which we had to pay up
front. In addition to taxi fares there were charges that
they owed to flop houses and bar rooms, and fines and
money advanced to them by the recruiters. It was not
unusual for a man to start work on a job with a sizable
charge against him. They were a profligate breed of
men, but they almost invariably worked off whatever
we had advanced to get them. In addition, they worked
until they had accumulated a bankroll they considered

...a little bucksaw work (1937)
Adamstown, Maine
Paul Charest

sufficient to provide them with a blow-out, on which they would quickly go broke, and have to start the procedure all over again. Many of them drifted from camp to camp and did not stay put in any one place for long. Occasionally some would adopt us and stay with us for several years.

There was one Russian known by the name of Charlie who stayed with us until he came to an untimely end. He was evidently a man of some stature among the Slavs. We financed him as a jobber for a few years as he attracted a large following of Russians and Poles and other Slavs who produced a lot of wood, but the wear and tear that resulted from their upheavals caused us to discontinue using him in that role. However, he had adopted us and stayed on with us, working wherever we needed him. He was of some value to us as he knew how to handle steep country. He called me Mister Bill, and I called him Mister Charlie. He was a disreputable looking piece of humanity with shaggy hair and a hideous glass eye, which startled everyone when they first came in contact with him.

A Mix of Years

He was as profligate a person as I ever knew. We paid him well, for he could log chances that were so steep and rough that no one else would consider them. When he settled up to "go out," he would have a substantial bank roll to play with; at least around fifteen or eighteen hundred dollars, which wasn't hay in those days. I do not know what he did with it, but within a week or ten days a taxi would deposit him at headquarters, broke and drunk, looking as if he had been through a hurricane, and very much the worse for wear. His glass eye would be missing: a happenstance which did not add to his appearance for he looked worse without it than he did with it. A week or so later we would receive a notice from some bar or flop house saying that they had Charlie's eye on which they had lent him money, and stating that they would return it as soon as they received whatever he owed them. In the dives that were haunted by lumberjacks, from Lewiston and Berlin to Albany, Charlie's eye was better collateral for a loan than a government bond.

He was alone, unclaimed by any relatives, and when he became too old to be productive we obtained his Social Security for him. We built him a shack at headquarters, which he shared with a big, white rooster that he had picked up somewhere as a companion. At night the rooster perched on a cross-pole of the camp that gradually took on the aroma of a henhouse. We were in the Adirondacks at that time. Our headquarters was quite a settlement as a number of our key men and their families lived there. An old bull cook took care of the place, and we had a horse that he and Charlie used to get up firewood. Outside visitors were greatly amused by the sight of Charlie riding the horse with the rooster, perched on its rump, riding behind him. That rooster was like Mary's little lamb — everywhere that Charlie went, that rooster was sure to go.

Each month Charlie's Social Security check went for food and rum in about an even split, and he and the rooster were happy. They lived an Edenic, worry-free life; one that can best be summed up by an expression which my father often used: "Blessed be nothing." One night, when he had been drinking heavily, the shack burned, and Charlie and the rooster burned with it.

We had one other man, Joe, who was about as profligate as Charlie, and he also stayed with us until he died. During World War II most of the native lumberjacks were lured into the ship yards, where they were paid high wages. Very few of them returned to the woods. Pulpwood was a product which was vital to the war effort, and our government and Canada arranged an agreement whereby we could import men from Canada by posting a bond that guaranteed their return. They formed at least ninety percent of our supply of labor, and Joe was one of the men who came to us under the bond. He was a wood butcher who could build almost anything with an axe and an auger, and was a valuable man to us. He built camps, sleds and drays, and he built several sluices which enabled us to get wood that was otherwise inaccessible. He built a thirty-three hundred foot sluice on Ascutney that was a marvel of engineering with curves and switchbacks to control the speed of the wood as it was sluiced down over the ledges of the mountain. We paid him well, and he always worked a long hitch before going out. His bank roll would exceed Charlie's by quite a margin. I do not think he blew it on wild orgies, but he lived in style and would end up broke, a long way from home, but sober. Most of the men traveled by car and taxi when they went out, but that was not Joe's style. He would charter a plane for his excursions. I think that he came from around La Tuque, for I once had to bargain with a bush pilot to bring him back from Lac-a-Beauce.

Joe was taken sick while he was with us and died in the hospital. Neither Joe nor Charlie had any relations; at least none that wanted to have anything to do with them. We provided hospital care for Joe and also a funeral service, burial lot, and stone for each of them. I think they would have enjoyed the send-off we gave them.

Only a very few of the men who left to work in the shipyards returned to the woods. We were dependent upon Canadian labor until we stopped logging in 1955. Mechanization — chain saws, tractors, skidders, and other heavy equipment — turned the lumberjacks into grease monkeys or equipment operators. They earn more money, but the cost of meeting government regulations and the financing of the equipment investment takes a large share of their earnings, and in terms of purchasing power it is doubtful that they are any better off than they were in the early days of the twentieth century; in fact, they may not fare as well. They are certainly not as stimulating or interesting as the men who let daylight into the woods during my time.

Past and Present

In the early years of our twentieth century, there was quite a wide gulf between the urbane life of the cities and the bucolic life of those who lived in the hinterlands. They were somewhat foreign to each other, and remained so until the advent of the automobile and better roads made frequent contact between them possible, initiating a period of social mobility. The stories of the hoaxes put upon the visiting green rustics by the quick-witted people of the cities contain a grain of truth, and the city slicker visiting the rural countryside was equally vulnerable to the wiles exercised by the country man when he was encountered on his home grounds. All of that gradually changed as the two began to mingle. The post-war period, starting with the decade of the 1950's, accelerated the mingling, and now those who choose to live in the less populated areas of the country are in many ways on an equal footing with the dwellers of the city. The movement to the rural countryside has been gaining speed for the last two decades, motivated at first by the desire for a second home and more recently by the urge for a place to escape the rat race and problems of the Great Society that are prevalent in the cities.

The invasion of the wilderness by the early land-hungry settler, armed only with a gun and an axe, which took place over two hundred years ago, has been duplicated in the last few decades by migrants from the cities. They are often resented and called flatlanders by the rural natives. The newcomers are intent upon escaping to a place which they consider more suitable to living. Instead of being armed with a gun and an axe, they arrive armed with a checkbook, and employ chain saws and bulldozers as their tools. They bring their amenities with them — or demand them — and those, combined with the technological changes that have occurred, are changing the tempo and customs of rural life to a way that is far different from that of the early years of the twentieth century.

Except for the family farm, which today has to be a capitalistic enterprise to exist, dependence upon the land for the essentials of living has disappeared. Federal and state regulations and high taxes combined with changes in technology and our orientation to a money economy have made the subsistence farm a thing of the past. Today country people meet their needs by purchasing instead of producing.

Almost any rural place that is not in a remote wilderness is a relatively short drive from a supermarket, a shopping plaza or mall, or one of the many fast food establishments, places of convenience that have left their stamp of sameness almost everywhere. If I should happen to go to the right place when I die, I would not be surprised to find a fast food emporium in front of St. Peter's gate.

Such establishments express only the outward changes that have taken place. More subtle changes have occurred that are apparent only to those who have been acquainted with the mechanics of living almost a century ago. The nearest thing we had to a fast food joint in those days was the roadside or curbside diner — often called a "greasy spoon." When you sat on a stool at the counter in one of those and ordered a hamburger, everything was above board. The counter man opened the refrigerator door — a refrigerator kept cool by ice — and pulled out some ground beef which he shaped into a patty and slapped on the griddle. Both you and he watched it, and when it was where you wanted it — rare or medium — he put it in a bun and placed it in

Farming Then (1915)
Benton, New Hampshire

School Then (1898)
Warren, New Hampshire

front of you. You watched the entire process and knew what you were getting.

Today, in a fast food palace, you order a hamburger and before you can even say rare or medium — they evidently never heard of either — something that is warm and wrapped in paper or is in a container is handed to you and that is it; a production-line hamburger. The first time you get a look at it is when you unwrap it. You have no idea of its contents or the process it has gone through; you can only wonder about them. It has to be accepted on trust with the concept that ignorance is bliss. To give the fast food palaces credit, one has to say that they feed a lot of people, and they do so cheaply and quickly, which seems to meet one of the two requirements of a society that is on the go; a full gas tank and a full belly, with little waste of time.

The convenience of the supermarkets has replaced the do-it-yourself producing and processing of the subsistence farm. When my mother planned a chicken pie she would inform us of the fact at breakfast, and someone would have to catch and kill a hen for her. The word "chicken," used in a culinary sense in those days, meant an old hen who had stopped laying eggs. Otherwise a chicken was something that had a lifetime of egg production ahead of it, and was too young to furnish any substantial amount of meat. The hens ran loose and a person would often have to spend from five to ten minutes or more chasing one around the yard to corral it. He had to grab it by its legs, hold its head on a chopping block, cut it off with an axe, and then start plucking feathers to beat hell in order to get them off before rigor mortis set in. My mother would then take over, and she had to gut it and prepare it for the pot. Today all that is necessary is a visit to a supermarket to obtain a chicken or any part of one that is ready for the pot or the skillet.

Even the simple process of retiring on a cold winter's night has undergone change. Today one turns down the thermostat, turns off the house lights by flicking a switch, crawls into bed, switches off the bed light, and is settled for a night's repose. Years ago, before electricity came to the rural places, settling in for the night was more time-consuming. The stove and its fire had to be put in order — the ashes emptied, the stove stoked with wood or coal, and the dampers adjusted so that the fire would last most of the night. That procedure was followed by extinguishing the lights, which were usually kerosene lamps. There was a knack to it. One turned down the wick, cupped his hand over the top of the lamp chimney and blew the light out by blowing on his hand. The same was done with the bedside lamp, and one crawled into bed in the dark. Arising on a cold and frosty morning and building or

Charles J. Gould,

Plymouth, N. H.

GLENWOOD STOVES AND RANGES A SPECIALITY.

renewing the fire consumed much more time and energy and was more unpleasant than the simple act of turning up a thermostat.

There are many subtle changes too numerous to mention. Most of them make life more pleasant and much less burdensome than it was years ago. It would be folly to consider returning to those days, even if we could, but such progress exacts a price. We are left dependent upon things other than our own resources. A sudden disaster, either man-made or a rampage of nature, that disrupts the things on which we are so dependent can suddenly plunge us back to the horse and buggy days. The intricate machinery and technology of modern life can come to a standstill, bringing most of us face to face with the fact that we are ill prepared to cope with the basics of living and survival.

Even the animals that provide us with sustenance have suffered a most pronounced change. On a subsistence farm with a small herd the cows were a part of the family. Each one could be quite individualistic, and they were given names and treated with some affection. Today cows are just part of a production line, judged only by their contribution to the bottom line. Instead of being allowed to participate in the enjoyable acts of nature, they are subjected to artificial insemination which must be most frustrating to them and also to their male counterparts. If they could talk, we would probably hear plenty.

Chickens and hens did not receive the affectionate treatment that the cows enjoyed, but they were allowed to run loose around the farm yard and enjoyed their freedom. Today they are closely packed in wire cages, and the eggs that they produce roll down conveyor belts to be mechanically sorted and packaged.

If we are not alert, we will find ourselves in the same category as the cows; members of a production line, being milked to pay for the whims of our legislatures and those who control them. There is already some evidence that we are being considered as such.

It seems to me that the march of progress that has taken place has made the future that our young people face more perilous than it was in my time. They are facing conditions and problems that are far different and more complex than the ones we had to contend with. From the time that they start their pre-school programs they are under pressures that we were not subject to. It is not as easy to land a decent job, or one that can be considered secure, as it was in my day.

Furthermore, the mores of today's society seem to frown upon physical labor and getting one's hands dirty, attributes that were considered to be assets when I was young. This is a more complicated age, one of

Photo by Vyto Starinskas, Rutland Herald

electronics and computers, worship of skills and status, and especially the bottom line. Even with the education that is necessary today, sudden developments can render one's knowledge obsolete and him with it. Today's technology can be beneficial to the bottom line, which may be why it is so excessively publicized, but it can also lead to massive changes that are destructive to the people involved.

We were not as subject to sudden changes in my active years, but there were two different occasions in which I was employed and associated in profitable ventures that were put out of business overnight. One was done in by plastics and the other by a ruling made by some bureaucrat in Washington. My salvation in each case was the fact that I had a working knowledge of other pursuits that I could turn to.

This experience probably makes me biased concerning the matter, but I believe the old adage that it is best to have more than one string to one's bow could prove to be beneficial in today's environment of sudden changes. Although it now appears unfashionable, the old Yankee trait of being a "jack-of-all-trades" gave a person the ability to adapt successfully to changing times, and it also gave him a high degree of independence.

The old saying, "It is more blessed to give than to receive," does not apply to advice. However, if I were a young person planning an assault upon the world today, I would make it a point to have at least a second string to my bow in the form of knowledge of more than one line of endeavor. Embarking on a long voyage, a good sailor usually carries a spare set of sails in his locker.

For those who enjoyed
A Mix of Years

A Country Life

by William S. Morse

Introduction by Noel Perrin

True stories of life on the farm and in
the woods of the North Country
in the early part of the century,
by one who was there.

Paperback, 136 pages, $9.95 (plus S+H)
Moose Country Press (1995)
ISBN 0-9642213-1-4.

What people are saying about

A Country Life

"If a rural New Englander lives long enough — I'd say 75 is the minimum acceptable, and 80 or 90 is better — he or she gets to be an old-timer. Bill Morse is a different kind of old-timer."

Noel Perrin
Dartmouth College

"Anyone who wants to learn what life was really like in northern New England in the early years of this century should read *A Country Life*."

Gary W. Moore
The Journal Opinion

"*A Country Life* will give you several hours of fun and quite a few chuckles."

Mel Thomson
N.H. Sunday News

"... a memory that dips into the early part of the century and brings up images clear as well water. Tales of outhouses and thunder mugs, of milking cows and swatting flies, of freezing in winter, sweltering in summer. Tales of farmers and lumberjacks, school teachers and blacksmiths."

Lois Shea
The Boston Globe

"... an old-timer tells what the 'Good Old Days' were *really* like."

Lisa Dale
Monitor Radio

Just A Few Stories
from A Country Life ...

Our life was not as harsh as that of my father's early days. One of the episodes that he related to me was of an experience he had with a terrific toothache when he was ten years old. His tooth became so painful that his parents decided it would have to be pulled. There were no dentists around in those days, and doctors were very scarce. If a doctor was not readily available people often resorted to a blacksmith who was experienced in pulling horses' teeth. In my father's case the blacksmith was the nearest. My grandfather gave him a silver dollar and saddled a horse that my father rode over the hills for a distance of several miles to the blacksmith, whose name was Glazier. Glazier made him take a drink of rum, set him on an upended block of wood, clamped some horse forceps on his tooth and pulled it out, after which he had him take another slug of rum. I asked if it hurt badly. My father said that it hurt like hell, but he felt that the ordeal of drinking the rum was worse than pulling the tooth. He was at a tender age to make the acquaintance of hard liquor, and he said that Glazier's rum was so strong and thick and raw it could almost be cut with a knife.

Dobbin

Webster defines a Dobbin as a slow, plodding, farm or family horse, and that is what most of them were. A countryman and his horse shared the tedious drudgery of toil and travel in all seasons of the year and in every sort of weather. They became quite dependent upon each other. A man took care of his horse, and there could be times when his horse took care of him. Cider flowed freely in those days. There were some who had a propensity for it, and there were times when a man might find himself some distance from home and unable to function properly. All that he had to do in such a case was to make it to his sleigh or buggy and Dobbin would take care of the task of getting him safely home. The horse knew the way; he did not need any guidance, and he knew what was expected of him. As a result of sharing their many vicissitudes a great affinity often developed between a man and his horse. There is the story of a farmer's lament upon the death of his wife. "God," he said, "I'd rather lost my horse."

Gramp

Geese are very large birds. They are primarily grass and vegetation feeders, and they are endowed with large strong beaks that enable them to get a firm grip on whatever they want to pull out of the ground. When they bite a person on the calf or his buttocks it hurts. Visitors learned to approach the house warily whenever the geese were around. Those which my grandfather had traded for were about as bad as a vicious dog, and we had to get rid of them. We tried eating a couple of them, but as I recall they were pretty poor fare. When I die and go to whatever place I am destined for, I hope it is one where there are no geese.

Horses

Old Lewis never drove anything but a wreck of a horse. I guess he wanted people to feel sorry for him. He traded horses quite often, and he had some trick of rejuvenating them just before he traded that made them look as if they were something. You could tell when Lewis was planning to trade, for his old wreck would begin to blossom. My father claimed that he fed them arsenic. He said that you could start feeding an old bag of bones a little arsenic, increasing the dose bit by bit, and soon have him fleshed out and looking like a new horse. The catch was that when you stopped feeding him the arsenic the horse quickly reverted back to an old bag of bones or, more likely, he died. It may

have been so. I can remember one time when Lewis stopped
at our place to show off a new horse that he had just obtained in a trade. He liked to brag about his trading prowess. The next morning he went out to the barn to feed him
and the horse was dead. My father and grandfather thought
it was a huge joke. Someone had beat old Lewis at his own
trick by trading him a horse that had been fed arsenic.

Logs

Another saw that they sent us was a circular saw
about twenty inches in diameter that was mounted between
two bicycle wheels so that it could be wheeled through the
woods. The saw was mounted at the end of a long handle
that was swiveled so that it could be used to cut vertically or
horizontally. Whoever put it together probably had a vision
of wheeling it up to a tree and sawing it down and then
turning the blade over and sawing the tree into pulpwood
lengths. It might have worked in a park, but it was of no use
in the rock bound hills of Vermont. We tried using it to saw
pulpwood in the yard, but found out that it was a lethal
thing. If the saw inadvertently hit the ground while it was
running, it would gallop away through the woods at a
terrific speed, gyrating wildly until it destructed itself by
hitting trees or stones.

Bender

Charlie, the jobber, was as bad as any of his men.
One morning, when he was drunk, he got mad at the cook
and went for him with a butcher knife shouting, "Me kill!"
The cook, whose name was Hebert, had a huge skillet on
the stove in which he had a mess of eggs and bacon frying
in sizzling hot fat. "Not me." he said, and he upended the
skillet, hot eggs, bacon and fat over Charlie's head. It tamed
him down and burned him so badly that he had to go to the
hospital. Hebert walked out, and we had to find a new cook
for Charlie.

The 18th

The rum runners were a wily bunch and were well organized. The cars which the agents captured were confiscated and sold at public auction where the runners promptly bid them off and put them back to work. A car loaded so heavily that it sagged to the axles would be vigorously pursued by federal agents, and it would lead them a merry chase over the countryside. When the agents caught up with it, they would find it loaded with bags of grain or some other innocent material. Meanwhile, a dozen cars or a couple of trucks with heavy loads of liquor would amble through town and along the route without any fear of pursuit. Country sheriffs and local police were only interested in their territory and were usually open to pay-offs.

✍ ✍ ✍

To order books from

Moose Country
Press

Call us
TOLL FREE

1-800-34-MOOSE
(1-800-346-6673)